Focus on
Families

A Reference Handbook

TEENAGE PERSPECTIVES

Focus on
Families

A Reference Handbook

Ruth K. J. Cline

ABC-CLIO

Santa Barbara, California
Oxford, England

Library of Congress Cataloging-in-Publication Data

Cline, Ruth K. J.
    Focus on families : a reference handbook / Ruth K. J. Cline.
      p. cm.—(Teenage perspectives series)
    Includes bibliographical references.
    Summary: Chapters discuss topics related to the family and include annotated lists of resources, such as fiction, nonfiction, and nonprint materials, organizations, and hotlines.
    1. Family—United States—Juvenile literature. [1. Family.] I. Title. II. Series.
    HQ535.C55 1989   306.85'0973—dc20   89-17937

ISBN 0-87436-508-2 (alk. paper)

97 96 95 94 93 92 91 90   10 9 8 7 6 5 4 3 2 1

ABC-CLIO, Inc.
130 Cremona Drive, P.O. Box 1911
Santa Barbara, California 93116-1911

Clio Press Ltd.
55 St. Thomas' Street
Oxford, OX1 1JG, England

This book is Smyth-sewn and printed on acid-free paper ∞.
Manufactured in the United States of America

Contents

Chapter 9: Child Abuse, 179

Preface

An old Chinese curse goes, "May you live in exciting times." Today's young people have grown up under such a curse—or blessing. They live in a world that is undergoing dramatic changes on every level— social, political, scientific, environmental, technological. At the same time, while still in school, they are dealing with serious issues, making choices and confronting dilemmas that previous generations never dreamed of.

Technology, especially telecommunications and computers, has made it possible for young people to know a great deal about their world and what goes on in it, at least on a surface level. They have access to incredible amounts of information, yet much of that information seems irrelevant to their daily lives. When it comes to grappling with the issues that actually touch them, they may have a tough time finding out what they need to know.

The Teenage Perspectives Series is designed to give young people access to information on the topics that are closest to their lives or that deeply concern them—topics like families, school, health, sexuality, and drug abuse. Having knowledge about these issues can make it easier to understand and cope with them, and to make appropriate and beneficial choices. The books can be used as tools for researching school assignments, or for finding out about topics of personal concern. Adults who are working with young people, such as teachers, counselors, librarians, and parents, will also find these books useful. Many of the references cited can be used for planning information or discussion sessions with adults as well as young people.

Focus on Families: A Reference Handbook is designed to provide young people with information on the topic closest to home— the family. Each chapter contains basic information on a topic related to families, along with annotated lists of suggested resources for further investigation.

Since the family affects all phases of our lives, it was necessary to limit the scope of this book. Chapter 1 examines what is meant by the word "family," and looks at how family structure is changing in the United States. Chapters 2 and 3 look at two kinds of families that are becoming increasingly common—stepfamilies and single-parent families. Chapter 4 explores the role of relatives, especially grandparents, in the extended family. Chapter 5 contrasts families with one child and families with siblings. Chapter 6 discusses adoption and what it means to be adopted, or to give a child up for adoption. Chapter 7 takes a look at the effects of finances on families. The last two chapters deal with troubled families—Chapter 8 talks about divorce and its effects, and Chapter 9 examines the issue of child abuse. (The issues related to substance abuse and their effects on family relationships will be dealt with in another book in the Teenage Perspectives Series.)

The resource sections in each chapter include fiction, nonfiction, and nonprint materials, as well as organizations and hotlines. Selection criteria included accuracy and readability as well as timeliness. Materials have been selected to be as current as possible; however, readers are advised to consult periodical indexes and guides to find the most recent information on each topic.

Most fiction entries are written for junior high through senior high school readers, with some books for younger children included if they are particularly poignant or have a universal appeal. Readers should be aware that books with protagonists younger than themselves may yet offer valuable information and insights. Most of the fiction entries have recent copyrights, but some older books were included because they have become "standards" for a particular topic. For example, Judy Blume's *It's Not the End of the World* was published in 1972, but is still referred to as a "must read" on the topic of divorce.

For the most part, entries are included in the chapter for which they are most relevant. The reader is encouraged, however, to skim through resource sections of chapters on related topics for entries that may defy easy categorization. For example, when researching divorce, it would be useful to check the chapters on single-parent families and stepfamilies for additional materials.

Most of the nonfiction entries are books, but some journal articles and government reports that are current or pertinent and not excessively technical have been included as well. The materials were chosen to present a balanced view on each topic, with the feelings and opinions of teenagers, parents, organizations, researchers, or society in general represented. The material had to have a recent copyright or else represent a viewpoint not found in the other sources.

Nonprint materials cited include films, videos, filmstrips, and audio cassettes. Films and videos are frequently available on a rental basis; many of these might be appropriate for a special class or church group presentation.

Information about organizations dealing with specific family-related issues is included in a special section following the nonfiction materials in each chapter. The information included has been checked for accuracy, but readers are warned that directors, addresses, and telephone numbers are subject to change. Hotlines and toll-free numbers are also provided in the chapters dealing with adoption and child abuse.

Many of the materials cited in this book may be obtained in school and public libraries. If you cannot find a reference in your library, you may locate it through interlibrary loan. Consult your librarian if you have problems locating a particular resource.

CHAPTER 1

The American Family

It was so strange to be back home, so strange. And my feelings about it were conflicted. Part of it seemed wonderful, but most of it didn't fit me anymore. I kept looking at that Raggedy Ann doll, with her perpetual smile, and thinking, the little girl who owned you is gone, kiddo. . . . My mom was waiting on me hand and foot, and that made me uncomfortable too. For the very first time in my life, I realized how spoiled I had been as a child. For the very first time, I saw how much they had invested in me. I don't mean money. I mean hopes, dreams, vicarious feelings, fantasies. My parents had lived their whole lives through me, and for what? I could never be what they wanted—because I could only be myself. And yet it was so touching.
Barbara Wersba, *Beautiful Losers* (New York:
Harper & Row, 1988), 123.

Rita has returned to her parent's home while she and her boyfriend have a trial separation. Looking at her old room, which is exactly the same as when she left it, makes her realize how much she has changed. Her parents have not changed any more than her room, and they have been hoping, in vain, that Rita would also be the same.

What Is a Family?

Our definitions of a family are subjective. They are based not only on our experiences growing up in our own families, but on images we receive from sources like television, movies, and books. Many older people still think of "normal" families as being like the ones portrayed during the 1950s and 1960s on television shows like "Leave It to Beaver" and "Father Knows Best," with fathers who worked at offices, mothers who stayed home and cooked and baked, and two or three children who always obeyed their parents and who loved and supported each other in spite of occasional mild squabbles. The family dog completed this picture of suburban domestic bliss.

In the 1980s and 1990s, the picture of the all-American family is very different. The rise in divorces, the increased percentage of women in the workplace, and growing numbers of never-married mothers have dramatically revised the traditional portrait. In 1989, according to the Bureau of Labor, only 5.9 percent of American families fit the traditional scenario of a breadwinner husband and a wife at home with two or more children.

Today's "typical family" might be a mother and her teenage son, or a father caring for his two young daughters. It could consist of two formerly married people, the children from their previous marriages, and the children they have had together. Many such families change character on weekends and during the summer, when children go to stay with their noncustodial parents. Even in a family consisting of a married couple and their biological children, both parents may have jobs or careers. All of these changes are forcing Americans to redefine their concepts of "family," as the statistics below make clear. In fact, the whole issue of "what is a family?" is interwoven throughout this book.

Terms

Biological parent. The genetic or birth parent of a child.

Nuclear, intact, or traditional family. Interchangeable terms for a family in which the adults are the biological parents and the children are natural brothers and sisters. (Getzoff and McClenahan, 2).

Parent or guardian. The person who is legally responsible for feeding, sheltering, and caring for a child.

Statistics about the Family

The U.S. Census Bureau statistics that compare the family structure between 1970 and 1986 give concrete evidence of change:

- The number of persons living alone grew from 10,851,000 in 1970 to 21,178,000 in 1986 (*Statistical Abstract of the United States, 1988*, 51).
- During the same period, the number of two-parent families with children under 18 declined from 25,532,000 to 24,630,000, while the number of single-parent families increased from 3,199,000 to 7,040,000. A "two-parent family" may include a stepparent (ibid., 49).
- Eighty-seven percent of single-parent families with children under 18 are headed by women (ibid.).
- The number of marriages per year increased steadily from 1970, when 2,159,000 couples married, to 1984, when 2,477,000 marriages were performed. During the same period, the number of divorces rose from 708,000 to a high of 1,213,000 in 1981, declining to 1,169,000 in 1984 (ibid., 83).
- In 1984, the remarriage rate for divorced women was 490 per 1,000 women (ibid.).
- The median duration of a marriage in 1984 was 6.9 years (ibid.).
- Between 1960 and 1987, the number of married women in the labor force increased from 19,799,000 to 31,282,000 (ibid., 373).

Women in the Workplace

Until recently, societal views of women and the family dictated that a woman had to choose between having a career and having marriage and children. The increase since 1970 in the number of families with both the husband and wife working indicates that society is adjusting to the notion of both marriage partners being employed.

The Job of Parenting

The advent of easily available contraceptive devices has meant that more families plan the births of their children. This does not necessarily mean, however, that the parents comprehend the responsibility of raising children or are prepared to cope with the problems that arise.

When 11- to 14-year-old students at the Fayerweather Street School in Cambridge, Massachusetts, were asked to describe the ideal parents, they included such things as "they would spend lots of time with their kids," "they would trust kids," "they would be helpful and kind and quite likeable," and "they would be nice but they would stick to their rules, which would always be reasonable" (Rofes, 6).

It is becoming more and more recognized that parenting requires specific skills and knowledge that many people may not have. Parents may be overprotective or overly strict. They may spoil their children or neglect them. They may try to control their children's behavior through nagging or embarrassing them. They may even abuse them physically, verbally, or sexually.

Most parents, however, are doing the best job they can in raising their children. Many books and workshops are now available to help parents, and more and more people are taking advantage of them to learn how to raise their children to become healthy, happy, and responsible adults.

Characteristics of a Strong Family

In the mid-1980s, researchers Nick Stinnett and John DeFrain conducted a study to identify the qualities that help families succeed. Three thousand families responded to their questionnaire, and six key qualities emerged:

- Commitment
- Time together
- Feeling appreciated
- Good communication
- Spiritual wellness
- The ability to cope with crisis

Commitment. In a strong family, members are dedicated to promoting each other's welfare and happiness. The family comes before career, friends, or other demands on time and energy.

Time together. Family members spend lots of time working, playing, and eating meals together and attending religious services. Strong families said the time together had to be sufficient in quantity, as well as generating good feelings.

Feeling appreciated. Members of strong families actively look for positive attributes in one another. The quantity of appreciation expressed to family members was greater than expected.

Good communication. Communication between family members creates a sense of belonging, clears up misunderstandings, and eases tensions. The responses revealed families were aware of practicing good communication and did not expect it to just happen.

Spiritual wellness. This quality was defined as a caring center within each person that promotes sharing, love, and compassion for others. Strong families express their spirituality in the way they live each day and by the values on which they base their decisions.

The ability to cope with crisis. This involves adaptability as well as skill in communication, focusing on the positive, and spiritual resources. A strong family provides a place for its members to be comforted, regenerated, and developed.

These qualities can be found in any type of family—nuclear, single-parent, or blended. They may even be found in a "family" comprised of nonrelated people who may or may not live together, but who support and care for one another and who think of themselves as a family. The new American family need not conform to any particular stereotype or standard structure in order to succeed.

REFERENCES

Getzhoff, Ann, and Carolyn McClenahan. *Stepkids: A Survival Guide for Teenagers in Stepfamilies . . . and for Stepparents Doubtful of Their Own Survival*. New York: Walker, 1984.

Rofes, Eric E., and the students at Fayerweather Street School. *The Kids' Book about Parents*. Boston: Houghton Mifflin, 1984.

Statistical Abstract of the United States, 1988: National Data Book and Guide to Sources, 108th edition. Washington, DC: Government Printing Office, 1987.

Stinnett, Nick, and John DeFrain. *Secrets of Strong Families*. Boston: Little, Brown, 1986.

Wersba, Barbara. *Beautiful Losers*. New York: Harper & Row, 1988.

Resources
for Finding Out about Families

The resources listed here deal with families in general and relationships within families in particular.

The Family in Fiction

Anaya, Rudolfo A. **Bless Me, Ultima.** Berkeley, CA: Quinto Sol Books, 1976. 248p.

In the New Mexico of the 1940s, young Antonio grows into manhood as his family enjoys the wisdom and magic of Ultima, his Grande. The Chicano family's customs and beliefs form a backdrop for the story.

Asher, Sandy. **Everything Is Not Enough.** New York: Delacorte, 1987. 155p.

Although his parents have worked hard to give 17-year-old Michael everything, he wants to find a life of his own and not follow the pattern handed down by his parents.

Burchard, Peter. **Sea Change.** New York: Farrar, Straus & Giroux, 1984. 118p.

The three sections of this novel tell of three generations of the same family, from the days of open carriages and summerhouses, to the homecoming of husband and father after World War II, to the present, when the overprotective mother worries about her liberated daughter in New York City.

Cohen, Barbara. **Roses.** New York: Lothrop, Lee & Shepard, 1984. 221p.

In this modern version of Beauty and the Beast, the father promises to deliver Izzie, his younger daughter, as an apprentice to Leo, the grotesquely disfigured proprietor of the Castle Florist shop. Izzie learns to draw larger circles around what was once a very small circle, with herself as the center.

Forbes, Kathryn. **Mama's Bank Account.** New York: Harcourt, Brace, 1943. 204p.

Written in the 1940s, this book about a close-knit Norwegian immigrant family living in San Francisco during difficult economic times was made into a successful play and movie, *I Remember Mama.* It shows how the family overcomes problems through family values.

Hall, Lynn. **Letting Go.** New York: Scribner's, 1987. 106p.

Casey, 16 and the last child at home, travels with her mother to show their prizewinning dogs at midwestern dog shows. Casey is beginning to feel her mother hovering over her and is anxious to have more freedom. Stranded overnight in a snowstorm, mother and daughter have a serious talk about "letting go," both admitting they enjoy their close relationship in the dog business but realizing that it won't last forever.

Hamilton, Virginia. **M. C. Higgins, the Great.** New York: Dell, Laurel Leaf, 1978. 240p.

Family life is the theme of this story of an Ohio hill boy who tries to come to a decision about the future of his family and their home. An unusual relationship develops between father and son.

Hannam, Charles. **A Boy in That Situation: An Autobiography.** New York: Harper & Row, 1977. 215p.

When the Nazis take his family's fortune, Karl, who had been popular in school, begins to suffer insults because he is fat, unattractive, and Jewish. The story focuses on how he adjusts to society and, more important, how he comes to be accepted for himself.

Houston, Jeanne Wakatsuki, and James D. Houston. **Farewell to Manzanar.** New York: Bantam, 1979. 144p.

Living in a relocation camp after the bombing of Pearl Harbor, a young Japanese-American girl relates her family's experiences and their fears, as well as her struggle between the Japanese culture of her family and the American culture of her friends.

Kenney, Susan. **In Another Country.** New York: Viking, 1984. 163p.

Six short stories portray family life through various crises and the resolution of grief and pain.

MacLeod, Charlotte. **Maid of Honor.** New York: Atheneum, 1984. 158p.

Preparations for her sister's wedding absorb Persis' entire family, to the extent that everyone forgets that Persis is playing in a state piano contest. A robbery makes the family look intently at each member for motives.

Miller, Sandy. **Freddie the Thirteenth.** New York: New American Library, 1985. 155p.

Freddie is the thirteenth child in a family of 16 but tells Bart, a boy at school whom she wants to impress, that she has just one sister. As Bart gets acquainted with Freddie's older brothers, she has to figure out how to keep her identity hidden.

Paterson, Katherine. **Come Sing, Jimmy Jo.** New York: Dutton, 1985. 197p.

When Jimmy Jo joins his family's singing group, he has to leave the security of life with his grandmother and learn new and disquieting things about his father.

Payne, Bernal C., Jr. **It's About Time.** New York: Macmillan, 1984. 170p.

Through their parents' old yearbooks, Chris and Gail are transported back to Christmas Eve, 1955, the year their parents met, and get to know them as young people. Other people in the girls' lives, including their English teacher and the family doctor, are also included in the time-warp scenario.

Sebestyen, Ouida. **Words by Heart.** Boston: Atlantic Monthly Press, 1979. 162p.

In the early 1900s, Lena Sills and her family have moved to a new town where they are the only black family. Papa's values come through in this story, which portrays a close family structure.

Taylor, Mildred. **Roll of Thunder, Hear My Cry.** New York: Bantam, 1979. 276p.

The Logans, a black family in Mississippi during the 1930s, struggle to maintain their dignity and self-respect. Cassie and her family maintain their enthusiasm for life in spite of bigotry and hatred.

Townsend, Sue. **The Adrian Mole Diaries.** New York: Grove Press, 1986. 342p.

Thirteen-year-old Adrian's diaries reflect his naive view of the world, especially of his parents and their rocky relationship.

Wersba, Barbara. **Fat: A Love Story.** New York: Harper & Row, 1987. 156p.

Rita is an only child whose middle-class parents have aspirations for her that include college. In telling her own story, Rita conveys her need to eat excessively, her interest in writing, and her infatuation with Robert Swann, which is replaced by her love for eccentric Arnold Bromberg—none of which are included in her parents' plan for her life.

————. **Beautiful Losers.** New York: Harper & Row, 1988. 149p.

In the sequel to *Fat: A Love Story*, Rita's story continues two years later. Rita and Arnold are living in substandard housing, without a decent income, and without the blessing of her parents. After a trial separation the couple gets married, and her parents accept the fact that Rita is going to make her own decisions and live her own life.

Wolitzer, Meg. **Caribou.** New York: Greenwillow Books, 1985. 167p.

In this story set during the Vietnam War, Becca's brother Stevie decides to become a draft dodger and takes refuge in Canada, going against his father's desire that he join the army.

Nonfiction Materials on Families

BOOKS

Benson, Peter L., Dorothy L. Williams, and Arthur L. Johnson. **The Quicksilver Years: The Hopes and Fears of Early Adolescence.** San Francisco: Harper & Row, 1987. 245p.

Search Institute conducted this study, which involved 8,000 fifth-through ninth-grade students and their parents, with participation solicited through churches and national 4-H groups in various regions of the country. The summary looks at the social context and attitudes, values, religion, and behavior of this group of young teenagers and their parents.

Bohannan, Paul. **All the Happy Families: Exploring the Varieties of Family Life.** New York: McGraw-Hill, 1985. 262p.

Although much of this book deals with divorce and its effect on the family, there are some chapters devoted to "Good Marriage" and "Well Families."

Haley, Alex. **Roots.** New York: Dell, 1977. 736p.

A story of family heritage and a search for family roots that took the author to a remote village in West Africa. The stirring television miniseries that was developed from this book inspired many people to find out about their own families.

Janeczko, Paul B., editor. **Strings: A Gathering of Family Poems.** New York: Bradbury, 1984. 164p.

Most of these recently published poems are written in a direct, unsophisticated manner and in a modern idiom. The poems are about relatives, husbands, wives, and children.

Klein, David, and Marymae E. Klein. **Your Parents and Your Self: Alike/Unlike; Agreeing/Disagreeing.** New York: Scribner's, 1986. 166p.

In this book for teenagers, the authors discuss how much of people's behavior, feelings, and thinking are determined by their parents' genes. Family life is discussed, along with friends, careers, and college.

Kolodny, Robert C., Nancy J. Kolodny, Thomas E. Bratter, and Cheryl A. Deep. **How To Survive Your Adolescent's Adolescence.** Boston: Little, Brown, 1984. 350p.

In this guide for parents, the authors strive to teach parents to think for themselves in helping their teenage children. The book is divided into four parts: General Issues, Problem Solving, Crises, and Positive Parenting Revisited. The authors stress honesty and clear communication but encourage parents to seek professional help when they feel the need. The Appendix offers addresses and telephone numbers of groups or organizations prepared to provide such assistance.

Lenero-Otero, Luis. **Beyond the Nuclear Family Model: Cross-Cultural Perspectives.** Beverly Hills, CA: Sage, 1977. 226p.

Based on papers presented at the World Congress of Sociology in Toronto, August 1974, the book presents a critique of the nuclear family model, an analysis of the coexistence of the various family types, and cross-cultural perspectives of the family. This work will be of interest to those studying theories of families.

McCullough, Bonnie Runyan, and Susan Walker Monson. **401 Ways To Get Your Kids To Work at Home.** Illustrated by Laura Hammond with Bonnie McCullough. New York: St. Martin's Press, 1981. 245p.

Realizing the home is a place for guidance and training, the authors give parents tips, principles, and strategies to prepare their children for independence and to help run the home more efficiently. In a survey of 250 children, over 97 percent felt they should work at home. The authors develop a plan for setting goals, assigning tasks, and giving rewards, including checklists for their ideas.

Packer, Alex J. **Bringing Up Parents: The Adolescent's Handbook.** Illustrated by Philip Stevenson. Washington, DC: Acropolis Books, 1985. 252p.

In this book for teenagers, the author discusses behaviors and expectations of parents and children and suggests strategies for better relationships.

Rofes, Eric E., and the students at the Fayerweather Street School. **The Kids' Book about Parents: Advice from the Real Experts for Kids . . . and Parents, Too!** Boston: Houghton Mifflin, 1984. 204p.

Thirty-two young people, ages 11 through 14, wrote this book to help others and themselves deal with parents. They also try to help parents understand children's and teenagers' points of view.

Stinnett, Nick, and John DeFrain. **Secrets of Strong Families.** Boston: Little, Brown, 1986. 288p.

A request for information in four dozen newspapers in 25 states resulted in responses from 3,000 families. The responses showed that strong families share six key qualities: commitment, time together, appreciation, communication, spiritual wellness, and the ability to cope with crisis.

ARTICLES

Comer, James P. **"Books for Parents of Teenagers,"** *Parents* 61, no. 30 (March 1986): 184.

Suggested reading for parents who want to know more about parent-teen relationships and the changes taking place in each other and society.

Hamill, Pete. **"Great Expectations,"** *Ms.* 15, no. 3 (September 1986): 34–37.

Men and women explain what they want from marriage and describe new arrangements for combining dual careers and children. The author talks about the search for the Great Good Place and young people who want to Have It All.

Joseph, Pamela B. **"The Changing American Family,"** *Social Education* 50, no. 6 (October 1986): 458–463.

Urging schools to present a current model of families for students, the author discusses the changes in the family and includes a bibliography about the family and its history.

Kantrowitz, Barbara. **"Three's a Crowd,"** *Newsweek* 108, no. 9 (1 September 1986): 68–76.

Reporting on the increasing rate of childlessness in this country, the highest since the Depression, the author describes interviews and surveys supporting the idea that while women used to think of having children and perhaps a career, now they have a career and *may* think about having children. Demographers forecast that as many as 20 percent of women now in their early to mid-30s may never have children.

Ludtke, Melissa. **"Through the Eyes of Children,"** *Time* 132, no. 6 (8 August 1988): 32–57.

Through the stories of five children in different parts of the United States, the author shows vividly how changes in family structure have affected the lives of children. Excellent photographs accompany the article.

Norton, Arthur J. **"Families and Children in the Year 2000,"** *Children Today* 16, no. 4 (July–August 1987): 6–9.

Using changes over the past two decades, the author predicts social, economic, and demographic circumstances between now and the end of this century, including later ages for marriages and childbirth, smaller family size, greater ethnic diversity, and increasing longevity of the adult population.

Nonprint Materials on Families

Alone in the Family

Type:	3/4″ video
Length:	13 min.
Cost:	Purchase, no amount indicated
Distributor:	Films Inc.
	5547 N. Ravenswood Avenue
	Chicago, IL 60640-1199
Date:	1976

A girl from a big family and a fatherless boy tell how their situations affect their lives. From the television series "Zoom."

The American Family: An Endangered Species (series)
Type: 3/4" video
Length: 10 programs, 9 min. average
Cost: Purchase, no amount indicated
Distributor: Films Inc.
               5547 N. Ravenswood Avenue
               Chicago, IL 60640-1199
Date: 1979

The American Family series focuses on a variety of family units through a series of intimate film essays. The series covers a wide social, economic, racial, and geographic range. All programs are available individually. Running times vary. Support materials available. Individual titles are family names except for number ten, "Share-a-Home."

The Baxters (series)
Type: Various video formats
Length: 5 programs, 22 min. each
Cost: Purchase, no amount indicated
Distributor: ABC Media Concepts
               1330 Avenue of the Americas
               New York, NY 10019
Date: 1978

A series about a typical American family and their complex personal and social problems, which demand thoughtful decisions in which the viewer can participate. The programs are available individually. Support materials available.

Because They Love Me
Type: Various video formats
Length: 31 min.
Cost: Purchase, no amount indicated
Distributor: Coronet Film and Video
               108 Wilmot Road
               Deerfield, IL 60015-9990
Date: 1981

Highlights the home life of a representative middle-class family, focusing on Jessie, the younger of two daughters. The video explores the effects that parental expectations have on children and stresses the need for learning new behavior. Support materials available.

Big Boys CAN Cry: The Changing American Man
Type: 16mm film
Length: 28 min.
Cost: Rental $17
Distributor: MTI Teleprograms Inc.
                  108 Wilmot Road
                  Deerfield, IL 60015-9990
Date: 1982

Examines how social and economic transitions have created changes in men's traditional roles and values. Case histories of a variety of family styles illustrate how both men and women are adjusting.

Building Family Relationships
Type: Various video formats
Length: 30 min.
Cost: Purchase, no amount indicated
Distributor: Films Inc.
                  5547 N. Ravenswood Avenue
                  Chicago, IL 60640-1199
Date: 1980

Phil Donahue narrates this film, which stresses trust, confidence, and a sense of belonging as the keystones of a strong bond between parents and their children.

Communications: Two's through Teens
Type: 16mm film or video
Length: 9 min.
Cost: Rental $29, purchase $210 (film); purchase $130
                  (video)
Distributor: BFA Educational Media
                  Division of Phoenix Films & Video
                  468 Park Avenue South
                  New York, NY 10016
Date: 1984

Introduces the importance of both interpersonal and public communication, using narration, music, and rapidly changing scenes.

Dave and Hazel: A Study in Communication
Type: 16mm film
Length: 28 min.
Cost: Rental $10.50

Distributor: Cashier's Office
                 University of Missouri
                 123 Jesse Hall
                 Columbia, MO 65211
Date: 1963

Focuses on how a family's lack of communication adversely affects the development of a healthy emotional climate.

A Day in the Life of Harvey MacNeill

Type: 16mm film
Length: 9 min.
Cost: Rental $8
Distributor: Filmfair Communication
                 10900 Ventura Boulevard
                 P.O. Box 1728
                 Studio City, CA 91604
Date: 1976

This film shows how a family can use free community services to help cope with unemployment or low income. Shows the use of libraries, health services, and agencies.

Exploring Problems

Type: 16mm film
Length: 22 min.
Cost: Rental $35, purchase $400
Distributor: Ecufilm
                 810 Twelfth Avenue South
                 Nashville, TN 37203
Date: 1985

A group of parents discuss ways they can bring their families closer together through family problems shared by the group. From the series Parenting: Growing Up Together.

Families

Type: 16mm film, 3/4" and 1/2" video
Length: 54 min.
Cost: Rental $55, purchase $550 (film); purchase $290
                 (3/4" video); rental $55, purchase $275 (1/2" video)
Distributor: Mass Media Ministries
                 2116 N. Charles Street
                 Baltimore, MD 21218
Date: 1986

Six vignettes explore the subtleties of family relationships and examine the conflicts that occur as individuals pass through life.

Family
Type: Various video formats
Length: 14 min.
Cost: Purchase, no amount indicated
Distributor: Wombat Productions
             A Division of Cortech, Inc.
             250 W. 57th Street, Suite 916
             New York, NY 10019
Date: 1973

The need for family remains throughout a person's growth to individuality and independence. The program probes the ties that bind and those that strangle.

The Family and Survival
Type: VHS and $1/2''$ video
Length: 52 min.
Cost: Purchase $279 (VHS), $179 ($1/2''$)
Distributor: Films for the Humanities
             P.O. Box 2053
             Princeton, NJ 08540
Date: 1986

Phil Donahue travels to three U.S. communities where particular events have drastically affected family survival, including a corporate town disrupted by frequent moves, a town where a major plant has closed, and a community stricken by farm foreclosures. From the series The Human Animal.

How To Raise Parents (2-film set)
Type: 16mm film or video
Length: 60 min. each
Cost: Purchase $1,400 (film); rental $150, purchase $450
             (video)
Distributor: Franciscan Communications
             1129 S. Santee Street
             Los Angeles, CA 90015
Date: 1985

Examines changes in family life and relationships through interviews with teenagers and parents.

Living with Parents: Conflicts, Comforts, and Insights
Type: 2 videocassettes, VHS, Beta, $3/4''$ U-Matic
Length: 40 min.
Cost: Purchase $149

Distributor: Human Relations Media
                 175 Tompkins #V212
                 Pleasantville, NY 10570-9973
Date: 1988

A live-action video in two parts: Part 1 is a dramatization of a teen party; Part 2 is an analysis of the conflicts and possible resolutions from Part 1. This video provides teenagers with concrete strategies for getting along with their parents.

My Main Man
Type: Various video formats
Length: 14 min.
Cost: Purchase or rental, no amount indicated
Distributor: Paulist Productions
                 P.O. Box 1057
                 Pacific Palisades, CA 90272
Date: 1976

The story of a black father and son's struggle to relate to each other, illustrating the theme that love heals all wounds and builds bridges between people.

My Mother Was Never a Kid
Type: Various video formats
Length: 46 min.
Cost: Purchase or rental, no amount indicated
Distributor: The Learning Corp of America
                 108 Wilmot Road
                 Deerfield, IL 60015-9990
Date: 1981

When 13-year-old Victoria takes a look back in time at some of the things her mother did as a kid, she realizes that a little understanding can go a long way in closing the generation gap. Available in a 30-minute edited version. Support material available.

Roots (12-part series)
Type: 16mm films (2 reels per part)
Length: 48 min. each part
Cost: Rental $18 per part
Distributor: Films Inc.
                 5547 N. Ravenswood Avenue
                 Chicago, IL 60640-1199
Date: 1976

A dramatization of Alex Haley's best-selling book, concerning the search for his family that takes him to Africa and through the slave era to modern times.

Searching Years (series)
Type:	Various video formats
Length:	11 programs, 15 min. average
Cost:	Purchase, no amount indicated
Distributor:	Churchill Films
	662 N. Robertson Boulevard
	Los Angeles, CA 90069
Date:	1973

The urgent issues of adolescence, as chosen by young people themselves, are explored in these programs. No answers are given; the programs are springboards into group activity. Available separately. Individual titles include: "Can a Parent Be Human?" "Mom, Why Won't You Listen?" "Wait Until Your Father Gets Home!" "Ruben and Gangs—Different Neighborhoods."

To Be a Man
Type:	Film and all video formats
Length:	43 min.
Cost:	Purchase $630 (film), $300 (video)
Distributor:	Coronet Film and Video
	108 Wilmot Road
	Deerfield, IL 60015-9990
Date:	1979

Using file footage and historical film, this presentation shows interviews with men in various life situations, while a relationship between one father and son shows male role modeling.

Organizations Concerned with the Family

American Family Society
Box 800
Rockville, MD 20851
(301) 460-4455
President: Kenneth Wayne Scott

Designed for individuals and organizations interested in improving the quality of family life in the United States, AFS distributes materials aimed at encouraging parents to spend quality time with families. AFS also gives regional, community, and national Great American Family Awards to families who uphold traditional values.

PUBLICATIONS: *Because Your Family Matters* newsletter (monthly) and *The Great American Family Builder* brochure, with activities for local groups (annual).

American Mothers, Inc.
Waldorf Astoria
301 Park Avenue
New York, NY 10022
(212) 755-2539
President: Ellen L. Ralph

American Mothers seeks to strengthen the moral and spiritual foundations of the American home and family, and to give the observance of Mother's Day a "spiritual quality representative of ideal motherhood."

PUBLICATIONS: newsletter (quarterly) and the *Literary Awards Journal* yearbook.

Family Resource Coalition (FRC)
230 N. Michigan Avenue, Room 1625
Chicago, IL 60601
(312) 726-4750
Director: Dr. Gail Christopher

A nationwide, community-based family support organization concerned with parenting and child development. Parent Action, a legislative advocacy arm of FRC, has offices in Chicago and Washington, D.C.

PUBLICATIONS: *Coalition Connection* (6/year) and *FRC Report* (3/year).

Family Service America
11700 W. Lake Park Drive
Milwaukee, WI 53224
(414) 359-2111
President: Geneva B. Johnson

The headquarters organization of a private, nonprofit, voluntary movement dedicated to strengthening family life, Family Service America directly serves agencies concerned with family counseling, family life education, and family advocacy services. A network of 11,000 professional staff is supported by over 10,000 volunteeers and serves 3.2 million people.

PUBLICATIONS: *Social Casework* (10/year), plus an array of books, brochures, and videotapes.

National Council on Family Relations
1910 W. County Road B, Suite 147
St. Paul, MN 55113
(612) 633-6933
Executive Director: Mary Jo Czaplewski

An international organization that links multidisciplinary family professionals who seek to advance marriage and family life through consultation, conferences, and dissemination of information. Members are encouraged to join the special-interest sections within the organization to promote networking and greater involvement. The council also maintains the Family Resources Database, which allows access to articles, books, and other information for researchers, students, librarians, and professionals.

PUBLICATIONS: *Family Relations* (quarterly), *Journal of Marriage and the Family* (quarterly), and NCFR newsletter (quarterly).

National Institute for the Family
3019 Fourth Street NE
Washington, DC 20017
(202) 269-3461
Executive Director: Donald B. Conroy

Seeks to strengthen American families by providing educational programs to adults, conducting research, and disseminating information on family education and ministries.

CHAPTER 2

Stepfamilies

"I've been thinking about this ever since Daddy married you and I wouldn't come here with him after you fixed up this room, and Daddy had begged me and I knew you were hurt about it. I didn't really want you to be hurt, Maggie, but somehow I felt good about it too. I knew it meant you cared about what happened to me—to all of us."

Sue Ellen Bridgers, *Home before Dark* (New York: Bantam, 1976), 147.

After Stella's father marries Maggie, Stella refuses to move into Maggie's house, even though the younger children do and are happy there. It takes Stella some months to leave the memory of her own mother and the little house the family had shared and move to Maggie's lovely home in town.

Historically, it usually took the death of a parent to disrupt an intact family. Stepfamilies were formed when a widow or widower remarried. As divorce has become more accepted in our society, the number of couples who dissolve their marriages and enter into subsequent marriages has increased dramatically. Consequently, more than a million stepfamilies are created each year. This chapter will help foster a better understanding of the stepfamily structure and the role of children in it.

Terms

Bonding. The physical and emotional ties that develop between people, such as parent-child love. Bonding evolves over time: it begins before birth for parents who anticipate the arrival of their baby, but occurs more slowly for stepparents and stepchildren who are introduced in quite different circumstances.

Half-brother or half-sister. Siblings who have one biological parent in common.

Stepfamily or blended family. A family consisting of two remarried (or living-together) adults, the children of each from former marriages, and any children they have had together in the present marriage (Keshet, 7). Stepchildren, the birth children of either adult in the stepfamily, may live either with the stepfamily couple or elsewhere, usually with their other biological parent.

Stepparent. The spouse of a child's biological parent. In most states, stepparents do not have legal rights or responsibilities regarding their stepchildren.

Stepsiblings (stepbrothers and stepsisters). The birth children from previous marriages of the parents in a stepfamily (Getzoff and McClenahan, 104). Stepsiblings are not biologically related to one another.

Statistics about Stepfamilies

- During the 1980s, an estimated 1.5 million second marriages took place each year (Keshet, 2).
- Sixty percent of second marriages include a parent who has custody of a child under the age of 18 (ibid.).
- About 1.2 million new stepfamilies are established each year (ibid.).
- In 1988, about 12 percent of all children under 18 were stepchildren ("Happy Step Father's Day," 4).

Death of a Parent vs. Divorce

Adolescents and children may be willing or unwilling members of a stepfamily, depending on many circumstances. One important factor is whether the remarriage resulted from the death of a parent, or from divorce.

DEATH OF A PARTNER
AND THE STEPFAMILY

When a marriage partner dies, the survivors have to deal with the mourning process and the finality of death. It takes a long time for the sad feelings and the hurt to go away. The children, as well as the surviving parent, may experience anger over the parent's death. Such anger may disrupt other relationships for a time ranging from months to years. Feelings of grief, anger, and abandonment are sometimes pushed below the surface and cause a new source of stress when they reemerge.

Children under the age of six are especially devastated by the loss of a parent. The concept of death is harder for them to grasp and they think the missing parent will return. Often they are not allowed to mourn or to attend the parent's funeral. They may be overprotected by caring relatives. The marriage of the surviving parent is a concrete expression of the reality of the other parent's death. Consequently, the new spouse may be greeted by hostility and aggressiveness.

Older children and adolescents may feel that the surviving parent should not date other people or that it is wrong to resume an active social life. They may feel that a romantic interest in another person is a betrayal of the dead parent. Often the dead parent is idolized and remembered as being perfect. If a marriage occurs when a child feels this way, the stepparent may be competing with a ghost—or an angel. Stepparents in this situation need to acknowledge the child's natural parent and confirm the parent's importance in the child's memory. The child needs to know the stepparent is not trying to take the place of the natural parent, but rather creating a new home with unique characteristics.

Children and adolescents who have lost a parent through death may have a different perspective of stepfamilies from children of divorced parents, since they do not shuffle back and forth from one parent to another. They may resent a stepparent for "replacing" a dead parent. Time, along with compassion and understanding on the part of both biological and stepparents, can help children to realize that, as Getzoff and McClenahan say, "a parent has a right to a second chance at marriage and happiness. That doesn't mean that she or he is betraying your dead mom or dad. Most of us need to love and be loved" (101).

DIVORCE AND THE STEPFAMILY

A divorce and the subsequent arrangements for the children influence how the children feel about themselves and their parents.

What have the children been told about the divorce? Do they perceive the events surrounding the divorce in the same way as it has been related to them? Do they blame one or both parents? What are the divorced parents' attitudes toward one another? Have the children been involved in the decisions about where they will live? The answers to such questions greatly affect children's attitudes about their parents' possible remarriages and the formation of stepfamilies.

Relationships within a Stepfamily

RELATIONSHIPS BETWEEN STEPPARENTS AND STEPCHILDREN

A remarriage takes place between two adults. Most of the time, the children are part of a "package deal." For many stepparents and stepchildren, the new relationship may feel artificial and strained.

The cruel or wicked stepmother is a vivid image in children's stories such as Cinderella and Hansel and Gretel. Yet this stereotypical image does not fit the reality of most stepfamilies. Many stepparents and stepchildren form strong and loving bonds. The formation of such bonds, however, is a slow and lengthy process. Neither person should expect immediate love and sharing. Trust, the basis for any good relationship, takes time.

Some stepparents may shower their stepchildren with gifts in an attempt to hurry love or make up for its lack. Children sense such insincerity and may end up resenting or manipulating the stepparent. Similarly, a stepparent who makes concessions in behavior for a stepchild and not for his or her own children—or vice versa—may appear as phoney and will probably lose the respect of both the natural and the stepchildren.

Seemingly small questions such as what stepchildren should call a new stepparent can lead to conflict and resentment. Adults may not want to be called by their first names, but the children may find it hard to call them "Mom" or "Dad." Some children and adolescents feel they are being disloyal to their birth father or mother if they call their stepparent "Father" or "Mother." And sometimes the birth parents object to hearing their son or daughter call a stepparent "Mother" or "Father." Finding a name that is comfortable for both children and stepparent helps form a basis for trust.

RELATIONSHIPS BETWEEN STEPSIBLINGS

A love-hate relationship is normal between children or adolescents who suddenly find themselves living with an adult and other children who are new to the family. Just as it is not unusual to have mixed feelings about natural siblings, it is natural to have conflicting feelings about stepbrothers and stepsisters.

There can be advantages to having stepsiblings. Sometimes it is easier for a young person to talk about feelings to someone who is near the same age and can understand. Stepsiblings can provide companionship during visits to noncustodial parents, which may help to relieve the tension that can accompany such visits. Stepbrothers and sisters can also be useful for helping with chores around the house, trading clothes, helping with homework, and giving advice.

Stepsibling relationships can also have disadvantages. Birth children may feel that their stepsiblings are replacing them in a parent's affection. If the stepsiblings live with the noncustodial parent, the birth children may be upset at knowing that stepsiblings see their parent every day. Jealousy and sometimes hateful feelings may result. Talking about such feelings can improve relationships and keep people from feeling alone. Stepsiblings may even find they share some of the same feelings.

Changing Roles in the Family

There are many natural ways an individual's role can change within a family. For example, an only child may become a brother or sister who has to share the parents' time and attention. The same is true of adding brothers and sisters through a parent's marriage. The oldest child has always been expected to act responsibly and has perhaps enjoyed special privileges. Now there may be older stepsiblings who will tell him or her what to do. Or the baby of the family acquires younger stepsiblings and loses his or her special place.

Children and adolescents alike may feel like they've been invaded when others move into their territory. When visiting the home of a noncustodial parent who has formed a new stepfamily, they may feel like outsiders. Adolescents may have a more difficult time than younger children in finding their role in a new stepfamily situation. Because they are more independent, they may resent a new authority figure telling them what to do. They may lose precious privacy, perhaps even having to share a room with a stepsibling. If their parent was single for a long time before remarrying, they may have had the status of a near-adult in the household, only to be "replaced" by the stepparent. It takes time to adjust to these new roles and to learn to share parental time and attention.

Making a New Family

Keshet believes the goal of the stepfamily is unification, becoming one functional family that will live in harmony together. She believes this is a process that takes two to four years from the time everyone moves into the same house. A stepfamily's development cannot be rushed; there are too many changes taking place at once. The two new spouses are developing their own relationship and getting used to being married. Whether the stepfamily came about as a result of a parent's death or divorce, the children may still be grieving and adjusting to dramatically changed circumstances. They must learn to live with a stepfather or stepmother while adjusting to a new relationship with the noncustodial parent, who may live in another city or state. They may be adjusting to a new school, or to sharing their house, yard, and school with new stepsiblings. (Keshet, 71).

Another aspect of blended families is that each member has his or her own family history and characteristics. Not knowing each other's "inside stories" may create feelings of being deliberately excluded, even when this is not the case. New family members may be unaware of long-standing family rules or procedures, leading to conflict and resentment. A lack of knowledge about each other's past can also lead to serious misunderstandings. Keshet cites an example where a mother became frantic when her new husband spanked her child. Because her first husband had beaten her and the children, the wife thought the spanking was a recurrence of that behavior (ibid., 75).

Everyone in the new stepfamily may not share the same last name, the same kind of humor, the same standards of neatness, the same traditions for holidays, or the same table manners. Such differences may seem trivial when children or adolescents are first introduced to their new family, but adjusting to the day-to-day routine requires tolerance, which precedes liking and then loving an individual.

Keshet encourages the use of family meetings as a way of communicating among all family members. She believes it is important that some decisions are reserved for adults, but she sees three functions of the family meeting: everyone has a chance to express an opinion, children have equal input on some decisions, and adults have an opportunity to remind children of expectations (ibid., 113). Such meetings can also be used to share feelings and family history, and to clarify family rules and agreements. For example, it may help new members to understand the background of a particular family custom or favorite food. Through such sharing and cooperation, the new blended family eventually creates its own routines, history, customs, and traditions.

New Babies in Blended Families

For children already in the home or stepchildren who live elsewhere, a new baby can be an exciting addition to the family. The baby can provide entertainment for the stepchildren, as well as drawing the focus of attention away from them. A baby may be a unifying factor in a stepfamily, drawing the members closer together.

On a negative note, some stepchildren find they are considered built-in babysitters and have no free time for themselves. A stepparent may devote more attention to the baby than to his or her stepchildren, leading to jealousy. Further, a baby may cause a parent to feel guilty about his or her absent children, who may in turn resent the new baby and its place in their parent's home and affections.

Sexuality in the Stepfamily

With the blending of unrelated people into one family, sexuality may become a loaded issue, particularly for adolescents who are just beginning to develop a sexual identity. Sex between a stepparent and a stepchild can have drastic consequences for all involved. Such incidents take place far more frequently between stepdaughter and stepfather than between stepson and stepmother. One study showed that stepfathers are five times as likely as natural fathers to molest a daughter (Leo, 73).

Even when sex does not take place, stepparents and stepchildren may have a difficult time knowing what behavior is and is not appropriate. The recent novel and movie, The Good Mother, dramatized what happened when a woman's lover did not understand what was and what wasn't an appropriate way for him to deal with her young daughter's natural curiosity. The mother lost custody of her daughter, and her relationship with the man fell apart. In a similar vein, an adolescent girl might find that "flirty" behavior that was safe with her own father is perceived by her stepfather as an invitation to sex.

Feelings between stepbrothers and stepsisters living in close proximity can also be troublesome. Sharing the same bathroom, eating together, and seeing each other every day may cause stepsiblings to feel attracted to or get a "crush" on each other. Usually these feelings pass as the siblings get used to the situation, see each other's faults, and resume their friendships outside the home. Sometimes it is not quite this easy and then all the people involved have to sit down and figure out what to do. Occasionally other living arrangements have to be made with the noncustodial parent or with another relative (Getzoff and McClenahan, 129).

Girls and boys alike should have information about what is appropriate behavior and what is not. They should also be able to talk to their parents about questionable or threatening behavior on the part of their stepparents or stepsiblings. If the parent is unapproachable or unwilling to help, school authorities are prepared to deal with complaints about sexual abuse (see Chapter 9).

Stepfamilies and Schools

The topic of school is a great concern to stepparents, according to a study by Manning and Wootten. They report that stepparents want teachers trained to include information about stepfamilies within the school curriculum for the benefit of all children. The stepparents would like educators and the public to perceive stepfamilies as "normal" and not "wicked" (Manning and Wootten, 234).

A second major concern indicated stepparents want teachers to be educated to be sensitive to the stress that children and their parents experience as part of the marriage-divorce-remarriage cycle. Teachers should know, for instance, about other resources within the community that could help children with complicated adjustment needs. Some schools sponsor special support groups for stepchildren, who are enthusiastic about the benefits (ibid.).

The third major concern involved the desire of stepparents and noncustodial parents to be included in their children's school life. Noncustodial fathers, for example, may want to see their children's report cards. Stepmothers may want to help with props for the school play. While schools are looking for ways to get parents more involved with their children's educations, a whole subpopulation is eager to participate.

Advantages of Stepfamilies

In spite of some of the negative aspects mentioned above, children in stepfamilies enjoy some advantages, particularly if they have access to both natural parents. They have twice as many listeners to hear their concerns, and they can get a break from one parent by visiting the other parent. Their circle of friends can be enlarged through the friendships of stepsiblings. They have larger extended families, counting grandparents, aunts, uncles, and cousins of the new family.

Children in stepfamilies may enjoy double holiday and birthday celebrations, since these occasions may be celebrated with both families. They may also enjoy vacations with both families.

Children in stepfamilies mature more quickly and learn more realistically about relationships (Getzhoff and McClenahan, 140). Because they have had to adjust to different ways of doing things, they know there *are* different ways that are acceptable. They are exposed to more different viewpoints, beliefs, and attitudes than children in intact families.

As Ann Getzhoff and Carolyn McClenahan write, "The stepfamily is a courageous and positive new family unit. It is not second-class. We will soon be in the majority . . . we are a different kind of family and we face different problems than other families. But we will survive and provide a second chance of happiness for millions of adults and children" (ibid., 142).

REFERENCES

Berman, Claire. *Making It as a Stepparent: New Roles, New Rules.* New York: Doubleday, 1980.

Bridgers, Sue Ellen. *Home before Dark.* New York: Bantam, 1976.

Getzoff, Ann, and Carolyn McClenahan. *Step Kids: A Survival Guide for Teenagers in Stepfamilies . . . and for Stepparents Doubtful of Their Own Survival.* New York: Walker, 1984.

"Happy Step Father's Day," *USA Weekend,* 17–19 June 1988, 4–5.

Keshet, Jamie K. *Love and Power in the Stepfamily: A Practical Guide.* New York: McGraw-Hill, 1987.

Leo, John. "Some Day, I'll Cry My Eyes Out," *Time* 123, no. 17 (23 April 1984): 72–73.

Manning, D. Thompson, and Marian D. Wootten. "What Stepparents Perceive Schools Should Know about Blended Families," *The Clearing House* 60, no. 5 (January 1987): 230–235.

Resources

for Finding Out about Stepfamilies

The Stepfamily in Fiction

Adler, C. S. **Footsteps on the Stairs: A Novel.** New York: Delacorte, 1982. 164p.

Thirteen-year-old Dodie and her new stepsister, Anne, gradually become friends as they investigate sounds of footsteps that may be those of two sisters drowned in a nearby marsh nearly 40 years before.

——. **In Our House Scott Is My Brother.** New York: Macmillan, 1980. 139p.

Thirteen-year-old Jodi tries to adjust to her father's remarriage, to her troublesome stepbrother, and to a stepmother with a drinking problem.

Bond, Nancy. **Country of Broken Stone.** New York: Atheneum, 1980. 271p.

Penelope's stepmother decides the family should leave the United States and take an old stone house in northern England for the summer. Fourteen-year-old Penelope has to sort out relationships in her new extended family while dealing with a sense of foreboding about their strange new home.

Bonham, Frank. **Gimme an H, Gimme an E, Gimme an L, Gimme a P.** New York: Scribner's, 1980. 210p.

Katie is an emotionally distraught girl struggling to cope with the haunting memory of a mother who deserted her when she was nine, a neurotic stepmother only nine years older than she who resents and emotionally abuses her, frequent moves, and an absentee father.

Bridgers, Sue Ellen. **Home before Dark.** New York: Knopf, 1976. 176p.

Stella, the 14-year-old daughter of a migrant farmworking family, learns to cope with the death of her mother and the remarriage of her father.

Danziger, Paula. **It's an Aardvark-Eat-Turtle World.** New York: Delacorte, 1985. 132p.

Fourteen-year-old Rosie, her mother, her best friend, and her best friend's father form a new family unit and find it takes a lot of work to make a family in a world of changing relationships. (A sequel to the story of *The Divorce Express*.)

Forman, James. **The Pumpkin Shell.** New York: Farrar, Straus & Giroux, 1981. 156p.

Overweight, 17-year-old Robin Flynn finds his once secure life completely turned around by his mother's sudden death, his father's remarriage, and his own strong attraction to his beautiful but hostile stepsister.

Gerber, Merrill Joan. **Please Don't Kiss Me Now.** New York: Dial, 1981. 218p.

A teenage girl struggles for balance in a year filled with conflicts: her mother's post-divorce antics and prospective marriage, her father's new and unlovable family, a steady boyfriend, the death of her only girlfriend, and the prospect of moving.

Kerr, M. E. **Love Is a Missing Person.** New York: Harper & Row, 1975. 164p. Available as a Talking Book.

Suzy Slade, the 15-year-old daughter of wealthy divorced parents, narrates a story dealing with racism, materialism, remarriage of parents, and sibling rivalry.

Klein, Norma. **Breaking Up: A Novel.** New York: Pantheon, 1980. 207p.

Fifteen-year-old Alison learns her mother is a lesbian while she is visiting her father and stepmother in California.

Lingard, Joan. **Strangers in the House.** New York: Dutton, 1983. 131p.

Fourteen-year-old Calum and his thirteen-year-old stepsister Stella must learn to adjust to their parents' marriage, in a story set in Scotland. Calum's father's second marriage breaks up, causing further distress.

McDonnell, Christine. **Count Me In: A Novel.** New York: Viking Kestrel, 1986. 173p.

Thirteen-year-old Katie has a difficult time adjusting to her new family situation, especially after her mother and new stepfather announce that they are expecting a baby.

Mazer, Norma Fox. **Taking Terri Mueller.** New York: Avon, 1981. 212p.

Fourteen-year-old Terri remembers life only with her father, but then she discovers that he kidnapped her from her mother after a divorce and that her mother is still alive.

Nostlinger, Christine. **Girl Missing: A Novel.** New York: Franklin Watts, 1976. 139p.

Erika lives in Vienna with her mother, her stepfather, her sister, and an aggregation of half-brothers, half-sisters, and unrelated grandparents. A mystery translated from German.

Oneal, Zibby. **A Formal Feeling.** New York: Viking, 1982. 162p.

Sixteen-year-old Anne Cameron, home from boarding school for winter vacation, comes to terms with her feelings about her mother's death, her new stepmother, and her own place in the world.

Oppenheimer, Joan L. **Gardine vs. Hanover.** New York: Crowell, 1982. 152p.

The selfishness of and hostility between two teenage stepsisters threatens to destroy the new family that their parents are determined to hold together.

Pevsner, Stella. **Sister of the Quints.** New York: Clarion Books, 1987. 177p.

When her stepmother has quintuplets, 13-year-old Natalie's life undergoes chaotic changes, and her family's roomy Chicago home becomes a huge nursery.

Pfeffer, Susan Beth. **Starring Peter and Leigh.** New York: Delacorte, 1979. 200p.

Sixteen-year-old Leigh has chosen to leave Los Angeles and her career as a television actress to move to New York with her divorced mother, who has recently remarried. The girl develops a positive relationship with her hemophiliac stepbrother Peter.

Platt, Kin. **Chloris and the Freaks.** New York: Bradbury, 1975. 217p.

This candid first-person narrative chronicles the dissolution of a marriage and its effect on a 12-year-old girl who is angry and feels helpless at her inability to preserve a comfortable and loving past. Her stepfather speaks for an adult view of marriage and divorce.

Smith, Doris Buchanan. **The First Hard Times.** New York: Viking, 1983. 137p.

Twelve-year-old Ancil struggles with conflicting loyalties between the memory of her father (who was reported missing in action in Vietnam ten years ago) and her new stepfather.

Terris, Susan. **No Scarlet Ribbons.** New York: Farrar, Straus & Giroux, 1981. 154p.

Rachel is happy at first about her mother's new marriage and about gaining stepsiblings as well as a stepfather. But resentment begins to build as her mother shares her time with the other children, and Rachel almost destroys the marriage.

Tiersten, Irene. **One Big Happy Family.** New York: St. Martin's, 1982. 390p.

Nina Stein leaves her own unsatisfying marriage and moves across town with Daniel, father of two. Together they take on the complex demands of work, children, stepchildren, parents, in-laws, ex-spouses, and their own relationship.

Van Steenwyk, Elizabeth. **Three Dog Winter.** New York: Walker, 1987. 144p.

A 12-year-old boy adjusts to his father's death, his mother's remarriage, and the integration of two families into one. The story takes place in the world of sled dog racing in northern Montana.

Wells, Rosemary. **None of the Above.** New York: Dial, 1974. 182p.

This book sympathetically portrays a 13-year-old girl's struggle to find a suitable life and future for herself while under the pressure of parental expectations and sibling rivalry after her father's remarriage.

Westall, Robert. **The Scarecrows.** New York: Greenwillow, 1981. 185p.

When visiting his mother and stepfather, Simon suffers a breakdown and is torn by his feelings of jealousy and betrayal. A chilling tale of what a person's imagination can do when hurt dominates his life.

Wolitzer, Hilma. **Out of Love.** New York: Farrar, Straus & Giroux, 1976. 146p.

Thirteen-year-old Teddy Hecht can't understand how her father's love can shift from her mother to his new wife, Shelley, and she is devastated when she learns Shelley is pregnant. Eventually, however, she and her stepmother develop a positive relationship.

Zalben, Jane Breskin. **Maybe It Will Rain Tomorrow.** New York: Farrar, Straus & Giroux, 1982. 181p.

A teenage girl feels helpless in the face of relentless changes in her life, including her mother's suicide, a new home with her father and his family, a new school, and a first love affair.

Nonfiction Materials on Stepfamilies

BOOKS

Anderson, Hal W., and Gail S. Anderson. **Mom and Dad Are Divorced, But I'm Not: Parenting after Divorce.** Chicago: Nelson-Hall, 1981. 258p.

Chapter 12 deals with "Stepparenting," Chapter 13 "Yours, Mine, and Ours: The Blended Family," and Chapter 14 "Re-creating Family Life after Divorce." The book emphasizes down-to-earth solutions and stresses the fact that children are not responsible for divorce.

Berman, Claire. **Making It as a Stepparent: New Roles, New Rules.** New York: Doubleday, 1980. 202p.

Recognizing the many changes in the configuration of the family today, Berman attempts to look at all angles of the stepfamily situation, including the needs of the various members of the family and the merging of two or more different life-styles, sets of rules, and methods of discipline.

Boeckman, Charles. **Surviving Your Parents' Divorce.** New York: Franklin Watts, 1980. 133p.

This book for young people takes a positive approach to changing family structures. Chapter 10 is devoted to stepfamilies, and includes advice on how to get along with new stepfamily members and recognize their feelings.

Booher, Dianna Daniels. **Coping . . . When Your Family Falls Apart.** New York: Julian Messner, 1982. 126p.

A guide for young people whose parents are in the process of divorce. Chapter 8 focuses on parental dating and remarriage and the acquisition of instant brothers and sisters.

Bradley, Buff. **Where Do I Belong? A Kids' Guide to Stepfamilies.** Illustrated by Maryann Cocca. Reading, MA: Addison-Wesley, 1982. 113p.

A reassuring book for middle school readers. Topics include Chapter 4 "Now You're a Stepchild," Chapter 5 "Stepfamily Problems," and Chapter 6 "How Does a Stepparent Feel?"

Capaldi, Fredrick, and Barbara McRae. **Stepfamilies: A Cooperative Responsibility.** New York: Franklin Watts, 1979. 154p.

After outlining the problems inherent in the stepfamily, this book offers positive alternatives for creating a cohesive, supportive family group. It is aimed at helping both stepparents and stepchildren to gain a better understanding of their problems while guiding them toward solutions.

Craven, Linda. **Stepfamilies, New Patterns in Harmony.** New York: Julian Messner, 1982. 186p.

Advice on a practical, down-to-earth level for teenagers dealing with issues such as family role conflicts and discipline problems. The book includes a sensitively handled section on sexuality in stepfamilies.

Drescher, Joan. **Your Family, My Family.** Illustrated by Joan Drescher. New York: Walker, 1980. 32p.

This book describes different types of families, including stepfamilies, and discusses advantages and strengths of family life.

Einstein, Elizabeth. **The Stepfamily: Living, Loving, and Learning.** New York: Macmillan, 1982. 210p.

The author draws on her own experiences as a stepchild and stepparent, plus numerous interviews, in this journalistic account of the problems "reconstituted" families encounter. Einstein believes people need information on quality of life in the stepfamily and what affects its survival, and she presents a positive outlook on these topics.

Espinoza, Renato, and Yvonne Newman. **Stepparenting.** Rockville, MD: Center for Studies of Child and Family Mental Health, National Institute of Mental Health, 1979. 63p.

Only a small number of stepfamilies have been included in the empirical literature in the last decade, making it difficult to generalize about results. The authors conclude that (1) stepfamily research is more difficult to do than any other kind of family research, (2) many people consider stepfamilies a solution to a social problem and not a problem, and (3) a subjective (and false) feeling prevails that we know enough about stepfamilies.

Felker, Evelyn. **Raising Other People's Kids: Successful Child Rearing in the Restructured Family.** Grand Rapids, MI.: Wm. B. Eerdmans Publishers, 1981. 164p.

Written especially for people, including stepparents, who are trying to help children who are not their biological offspring. Chapter 3 covers discipline, and Chapter 4 is "Maintaining Relationships with the Biological Family."

Gardner, Richard. **The Boys and Girls Book about Stepfamilies.** New York: Bantam, 1982. 368p.

In this warm and honest book, the author, a medical doctor, provides reassuring answers to many of the important questions children ask about stepfamilies. The emphasis is on being honest about feelings and learning to communicate them in appropriate ways.

Getzoff, Ann, and Carolyn McClenahan. **Stepkids: A Survival Guide for Teenagers in Stepfamilies . . . and for Stepparents Doubtful of Their Own Survival.** New York: Walker, 1984. 171p.

Written especially for teenagers, this guide gives practical suggestions on how to cope with various types of stepparents and how to get along with stepbrothers and stepsisters. Chapter 14 discusses "Parents in a Homosexual Relationship." Appendix II includes "Nine Ways for Stepparents and Stepkids To Become Friends."

Gilbert, Sara. **Trouble at Home.** New York: Lothrop, Lee & Shepard, 1981. 191p.

Written particularly for teenagers and intended to help them cope with family changes, this book deals with stepfamilies and how and where to get help.

Gorman, Tony. **Stepfather.** Boulder, CO: Gentle Touch Press, 1983. 172p.

The author presents the personal stories of men, their spouses, and the children involved in stepparent families.

Gruber, Ellen J. **Stepfamilies: A Guide to the Sources and Resources.** New York: Garland, 1986. 122p.

The books, articles, and the few dissertations cited in this annotated bibliography were written from 1980 to 1984, with a few earlier works included for their unique ideas. One section of the bibliography is intended for parents and one for teenagers.

Hyde, Margaret O. **My Friend Has Four Parents.** New York: McGraw-Hill, 1981. 120p.

This book for young readers offers excellent help for parents who are guiding their children through the transition from divorce to remarriage.

Jackson, Michael, and Jessica Jackson. **Your Father's Not Coming Home Anymore.** New York: Richard Marek, 1981. 320p.

This work is based on a collection of interviews with young people between the ages of 13 and 21 whose parents have divorced. The authors were teenagers when they wrote the book.

Jensen, Larry Cyril, and Janet Mitchell Jensen. **Stepping into Stepparenting: A Practical Guide.** Palo Alto, CA: R & E Research Associates, 1981. 139p.

Being a stepparent is a complex challenge. This guide is designed to provide answers to questions about the introductory stage, consequences of decisions, leadership through love, and living with differences.

Kalter, Suzy. **Instant Parent: A Guide for Stepparents, Part-Time Parents and Grandparents.** New York: A & W Publishers, 1979. 268p.

The author discusses common concerns of "instant parents," as well as their relationships with young people.

Keshet, Jamie K. **Love and Power in the Stepfamily: A Practical Guide.** New York: McGraw-Hill, 1987. 231p.

Realizing that previous parenting experience is not enough to prepare for the maze of stepfamily life, Keshet provides specific strategies for making the stepfamily work. The author claims the stepfamily follows three stages: acceptance, authority (the hardest stage), and affection (the happiest stage) and presents a chapter on each of these.

Lorimer, Anne, with Philip M. Feldman. **Remarriage: A Guide for Singles, Couples, and Families.** Philadelphia: Running Press, 1980. 158p.

The last section of this book is devoted to stepfamilies and discusses how parents can prepare children for the remarriage and for their new role as stepchildren.

Maddox, Brenda. **The Half-Parent: Living with Other People's Children.** New York: M. Evans, 1975. 196p.

This book includes ideas on childrearing and on relationships between stepparents and children.

Robson, Bonnie. **My Parents Are Divorced Too: Teenagers Talk about Their Experiences and How They Cope.** New York: Everest House, 1980. 208p.

Robson presents a report on interviews with young people that explore their understanding of their parents' divorces and remarriage issues.

Rofes, Eric E., and the students at Fayerweather Street School. **The Kid's Book of Divorce: By, for and about Kids.** Lexington, MA: Lewis Publishing, 1981. 123p.

Written by 20 students of a Cambridge, Massachusetts, school, the book is an open and practical guide to children's feelings about divorce and stepparenting.

Rowland, Peter. **Saturday Parent: A Book for Separated Families.** New York: Continuum, 1980. 143p.

The author interviewed many noncustodial parents who see the children "only on Saturday." He concludes that it is important and worthwhile for noncustodial parents to stay in touch with their children even though they no longer live together.

Sands, Melissa. **The Second Wife's Survival Manual.** New York: Berkley Books, 1982. 247p.

Chapter 10 contains strategies for stepparenting.

Savage, Karen, and Patricia Adams. **The Good Stepmother: A Practical Guide.** New York: Crown, 1988. 213p.

A discussion of such issues as money, sex, the ex-wife, and the stages that stepfamilies go through from courtship to the moment stepchildren leave home. Chapter 9, "Adolescence," is especially pertinent.

Sobol, Harriet Langsam. **My Other Mother, My Other Father.** New York: Macmillan, 1979. 34p.

In this book for young readers, a 12-year-old girl whose parents have divorced and remarried discusses the complexities of her new larger family.

Spann, Owen, and Nanci Spann. **Your Child? I Thought It Was My Child!** Pasadena, CA: Ward Ritchie Press, 1977. 176p.

Discusses stepchildren in the United States and the issues that remarriage brings up.

Thomson, Helen. **The Successful Stepparent.** New York: Harper & Row, 1966. 237p.

Although an older copyright, the book portrays a timeless sense of human feelings and human behavior. It espouses the philosophy that stepparents as much as children are entitled to understanding and the right to feelings and failings.

Troyer, Warner. **Divorced Kids.** New York: Harcourt Brace Jovanovich, 1980. 175p.

Presents a child's view of divorce, with children speaking of pain, bewilderment, loss of innocence, and lies they were told, as well as coping and their new lives with stepparents.

Turow, Rita. **Daddy Doesn't Live Here Anymore.** Matteson, IL: Greatlakes Living Press, 1977. 196p.

Includes a section on remarriage and children of divorced parents and on the trauma of divorce itself.

Visher, Emily B., and John Visher. **Stepfamilies: A Guide to Working with Stepparents and Stepchildren.** New York: Brunner/Mazel, 1979. 280p.

A psychiatrist and a psychologist write about the practical workings of stepfamilies.

————. **How To Win as a Stepfamily.** New York: Dembner Books, 1982. 196p.

The Vishers give specific advice for stepparents and stepchildren.

ARTICLES

Berman, Claire. **"When He Has Kids and She Doesn't . . . Yet,"** *Ms.* 13, no. 8 (February 1985): 36–37.

This article discusses what happens when a childless woman marries a man who is the father of children from a previous marriage, and whether they should have a mutual child.

Children's Express. **"Kids Compare Notes,"** *Ms.* 13, no. 8 (February 1985): 46–49.

A roundtable discussion among stepchildren who talk about the positives and negatives in their situations, including the trauma of life before the divorce.

Hyman, Beverly. **"A Five-Year Plan To Woo My Stepdaughters,"** *Ms.* 13, no. 8 (February 1985): 38–39.

A new stepmother relates her experience with her daughter and her husband's two young daughters who felt they were in direct competition with her for the father's love and attention.

Jarmulowski, Vicki. **"The Blended Family: Who Are They?"** *Ms.* 13, no. 8 (February 1985): 33–34.

Using the term "blended family" instead of stepfamily, the author describes the impact these families are having on every U.S. institution, from the greeting card industry to schools to stepchildren in the wedding ceremony. The article cites a research study that showed loyalty conflicts are usually the result of a stepparent's trying to assume a parent's role prematurely.

Lawlor, Julia. **"Happy Step Father's Day,"** *USA Weekend,* 17–19 June 1988, 4–5.

Lawlor discusses the move to make a special day for stepfathers since over 1,300 new stepfamilies are formed each day in the United States.

Maglin, Nan Bauer. **"It Could Not Be More Complicated,"** *Ms.* 13, no. 8 (February 1985): 40–45.

This article portrays the confusion in the mind of a professed urban, feminist, working woman who had an adopted daughter and who married a man with two biological daughters and an adopted son.

Manning, D. Thompson, and Marian D. Wootten. **"What Stepparents Perceive Schools Should Know about Blended Families,"** *Clearing House* 60, no. 5 (January 1987): 230–235.

Based on discussions with a sample of participants from a New Orleans chapter of the Stepfamily Association of Louisiana, this study outlines concerns stepparents have about their communication with schools, including assumptions about stepfamilies based upon stereotypes. The participants wish teachers had more knowledge of stepfamily issues and would incorporate some of these issues into the curriculum for all children.

Pierson, Dorothy A. **"Issues Confronting Adolescents in Stepfamilies,"** *The ALAN Review* 9, no. 3 (Spring 1982): 31–34.

Noting that, in 1900, 80 percent of stepchildren in the United States were from homes originally dissolved by death, the author describes changes in family patterns as depicted in literature. Pierson raises nine issues relating to the adolescent in stepfamilies, with illustrations from literature to show how the issues are treated.

Strother, JoAnna, and Ed Jacobs. **"Adolescent Stress as It Relates to Stepfamily Living: Implications for School Counselors,"** *The School Counselor* 32, no. 2 (November 1984): 97–103.

Although they used a small sample of stepchildren for their study, the authors discovered stress among stepchildren was no greater than stress among adolescents in nuclear families.

Nonprint Materials on Stepfamilies

The Bridge of Adam Rush
Type:	1/2″ video
Length:	47 min.
Cost:	Rental $12
Distributor:	Time-Life Video
	Time & Life Building
	1271 Avenue of the Americas
	New York, NY 10020
Date:	1975

In the early 1800s, 12-year-old Adam leaves a cozy Philadelphia home for rural life on a farm with his new stepfather. From the Teenage Years series.

Step Family
Type:	16mm color film
Length:	13 min.
Cost:	Rental $11
Distributor:	Centron Films
	108 Wilmot Road
	Deerfield, IL 60015-9990
Date:	1981

The film explores the positive elements and stresses of remarried couples and their children. From the series Family Life: Transitions in Marriage (A Case History).

Step Parent
Type: 16mm color film
Length: 20 min.
Cost: Rental $13
Distributor: American Association for Counseling and Development
5999 Stevenson Avenue
Alexandria, VA 22306
Date: 1981

Through vignettes portraying a variety of stepfamily situations and relationships, the film addresses issues pertinent to stepparenting.

Stepdancing: A Portrait of a Remarried Family
Type: 16mm film or video
Length: 27 min.
Cost: Purchase $495 (film), $395 (video)
Distributor: Pyramid Film and Video
Box 1048
Santa Monica, CA 90406
Date: 1987

An 11-year-old, his divorced parents, and his stepparents honestly articulate and warmly display the frustrations, emotions, and love in a blended family relationship.

The Stepparent
Type: Various video formats
Length: 29 min.
Cost: Rental or purchase, no amount indicated
Distributor: Michigan Media
University of Michigan
400 Fourth Street
Ann Arbor, MI 48109
Date: 1971

A University of Michigan psychologist views the contemporary stepfamily with insight and understanding in an effort to reverse society's stereotype of the "cruel stepparent."

Stepparenting: New Families, Old Ties
Type: Various video formats
Length: 25 min.

Cost: Purchase, no amount indicated
Distributor: Polymorph Films
               118 South Street
               Boston, MA 02111
Date: 1977

Members of a stepparent support group discuss their initial feelings
of insecurity, conflicts on childrearing practices, and confusion as to
who has authority. The program also documents scenes from lives of
stepfamilies.

Stepparenting Issues

Type: Various video formats
Length: 20 min.
Cost: Purchase, no amount indicated
Distributor: Human Services Development
               1616 Soldiers Field Road
               Boston, MA 02135
Date: 1981

The vignettes in this program present some of the common situations
and frustrations encountered in stepparenting. Support materials
available.

Organizations Concerned with Stepfamilies

Remarried Parents, Inc.

102-20 67th Drive
Forest Hills, NY 11375
(718) 459-2011
Founder: Jack Pflaster

The group sponsors social activities, monthly meetings, lectures,
and therapy groups for parents working toward the success of
second marriages.

PUBLICATION: Newsletter (monthly).

Step Family Foundation

333 West End Avenue
New York, NY 10023
(212) 877-3244
Executive Director: Jeannette Lofas

Intended for remarried persons with children, interested
professionals, and divorced persons, the foundation gathers

information on the stepfamily and stepfamily relationships, holds group counseling sessions for stepfamilies, and organizes lectures and workshops. The foundation is also a clearinghouse where materials such as books and audiocassettes can be purchased.

PUBLICATION: Newsletter (quarterly).

Stepfamily Association of America (SAA)
602 E. Joppa Road
Baltimore, MD 21204
(301) 823-7570
Executive Director: Jane R. Maytin
Founded in 1979 to act as a support network for stepparents, remarried parents and their children, and single people who contemplate marriage to a partner with children, the SAA provides education, children's services, and referral services, and conducts mutual help groups.

PUBLICATIONS: *The Stepfamily Bulletin* (quarterly); a manual, *Learning to Step Together*; and a bibliography of books, articles, and research reports on stepfamily issues.

CHAPTER 3

Single-Parent Families

> That night I began thinking that just at certain times I
> would like to have a father.... The funny thing is that I
> can't imagine Mom with a husband ... I guess because for
> me to have a father, I wouldn't have to be any different.
> But for her to have a husband, I guess I imagine she would
> have to stop wearing blue jeans and having her hair in a
> pony tail and have to do more regular things.
>
> Norma Klein, *Mom, the Wolf Man and Me*,
> (New York: Pantheon, 1972), 27.

Brett, wise beyond her 11 years, and her magazine photographer
mother have a comfortable and fun life without a husband and father.
It is a nuisance when Brett changes schools and has to explain to
people again that her mother was never married, but she handles the
responses with gusto. Published in 1972, *Mom, the Wolf Man and Me*
is a forerunner of books about the bright, illegitimate child.

> "Listen. I'm thirty-eight years old. Single. I date. I have a
> right to go out. It may upset you, but I do go out. I just don't
> do it while you're home. We have enough to adjust to
> already with our new life." "I like our new life just the way
> it is," I (Phoebe) tell him. "We don't need anybody else."
> He shakes his head but says nothing.
>
> I bite my fingernail. "I just don't want you to bring home a
> wicked stepmother some day ... and no mean stepsisters.
> Promise." He rumples my hair. "Don't give me that Cin-
> derella number." ... He's really a good guy.
>
> Paula Danziger, *The Divorce Express* (New York:
> Dell, 1982), 27.

Since the divorce, Phoebe lives with her father during the week and commutes to New York City on weekends to be with her mother. The above passage is from her conversation with her father over dinner, which indicates she is happy to have him to herself. The thought of expanding the family is unappealing to her.

A single-parent family consists of a biological or adoptive parent and the child or children who live in his or her household. Single-parent families may form as a result of:

> divorce or separation
>
> the death of a parent
>
> unplanned, illegitimate births, often to teenage mothers
>
> planned birth by a single woman
>
> adoption by a single woman or man

Statistics about Single-Parent Families

- Twenty percent of all American children lived in single-parent households in 1986 (Bianchi and Seltzer, 43).
- Of the children of divorced parents, over half see their absent parent fewer than one time per month. One-third never see their father (ibid.).
- It is estimated 42 percent of white children and 86 percent of black children will live in a single-parent household sometime during their youth (ibid.).
- Experts predict that one out of every three families, possibly even one out of two, will be headed by a single parent in 1990. (Gelman, et al., 42).
- Nearly 90 percent of the nation's one-parent households are headed by women (ibid., 43).

Divorce and Separation

Divorce is the single biggest cause of single-parent families. In addition, single-parent families may form as a result of parents separating, where a divorce is anticipated in the future or the separation becomes a permanent arrangement. Although separation can occur without the same legal arrangements as divorce, the effects on the children can be similar, with one parent having effective custody (see Chapter 8 for more information on divorce).

Death

The death of a parent creates a different kind of family crisis than divorce. The finality of death, the stages of grief, and the survivors' efforts to resume a normal life take their toll on all family members. The cause of death, whether illness, accident, war, or suicide, also affects the way family members handle their situation and the support they receive from relatives and the community. Death by suicide, in particular, is often accompanied by feelings of guilt on the part of surviving family members and may result in a longer healing time.

Sometimes friends or other relatives hope to protect children from the reality of death by shielding them from the mourning process and the sights and sounds of the funeral. This may be harmful, especially to a young child who may anticipate his or her parent's return and who feels abandoned instead. Honesty and compassion, with the surviving parent answering questions in a straightforward manner, can make it easier for children to accept their loss. Sometimes children or other family members require professional therapy in order to heal and get on with the business of living.

Unmarried Mothers

Societal response to illegitimate births, particularly where a mother decides to keep her baby, have changed greatly in recent years. This is partly due to the visibility of divorced women who are raising their children alone.

- One-parent families maintained by a never-married mother increased from 5.4 percent in 1970 to 28.1 percent in 1984 (Gelman, et al., 46).
- Half of all black children live in single-parent, female-headed homes. Eight out of ten of these families in inner cities live in poverty ("Mothers Raising Mothers," 24).
- By age 20, nearly 40 percent of white girls and 63 percent of black girls become pregnant. Observers have noticed a drop in these statistics in the last few years (Levine et al., 67).

- In some cities, 80 to 90 percent of births to black teenagers are out of wedlock (ibid.).

TEENAGE MOTHERS

A teenager who becomes a mother and decides to keep her child faces difficult tasks in addition to continuing her own intellectual and physical development, including:

continuing school to graduation

providing for herself and her child

recognizing her potential for employment skills

taking care of the needs of her child, often without adequate maturity to be a parent

Some teenage mothers remain in their parents' homes, with the grandparents essentially becoming the parents of the new baby. In such cases the young mother may act more like a sister to the baby and not assume much responsibility for it.

PLANNED SINGLE PARENTHOOD

The other category of single, never-married mothers includes women in their late twenties to thirties, many of whom have professional careers. In 1978, over 40,000 babies were born to single women in their thirties, a 15 percent increase from ten years earlier (Merritt and Steiner, 5). Some of these babies are conceived through artificial insemination, either through an individual donor known to the mother or through a sperm bank. Or a woman may choose to ask a man to father her child, agreeing beforehand on the extent of the father's involvement and obligations. The question of how such children acknowledge their parentage has not been solved, and the effects of such conception on a child's social and intellectual development are unclear. (Kantrowitz et al., 67). Other women (and some men) choose to have a child by adoption.

Whether the mother is a teenager with an unexpected pregnancy or a career woman who has planned to have a child, support from family and friends is crucial. The stress of raising a child alone, providing emotional as well as physical support, and making all the decisions necessary for a family requires a strong person with a good support system.

Poverty and the Single-Parent Family

- Fifty-four percent of single-parent families were living below the poverty line in 1983, compared with 18 percent for all families with children. For families headed by females, the figure was 47 percent, compared with 19 percent for families headed by males. (Gelman, et al., 43.)
- More than half of black families fall into poverty after a marital breakup, compared to a quarter of white families (ibid.).
- Sixty-eight percent of black children in single-parent households are poor, versus 22 percent of all children in the United States (ibid.).

Single-parent, female-headed families are a major factor in what has been called "the feminization of poverty" (ibid.). There are several reasons for this growing phenomenon:

1. Women earn less than men due to inequities in the marketplace.
2. Traditionally, women have had fewer working skills to offer, and they are frequently paid less for those skills they possess. Many women work in what is called the "pink- collar ghetto," in low-paying service jobs such as waitressing.
3. Cutbacks in social welfare programs have aggravated the problem (ibid.).

Many divorced women and their children are forced by reduced circumstances to relocate to more affordable housing, usually within two years of a divorce. Such a move heightens a family's sense of loss. Many single fathers, on the other hand, are in higher-paying positions and can afford the housing and help to make life easier for themselves and the children.

In most states, courts have become more rigorous in requiring and enforcing child support when either single fathers or single mothers are straining financially to support their families. The Child Support Enforcement Act of 1984 gave states the right to garnishee a parent's wages if he or she is delinquent with child support payments.

Families headed by teenage mothers are especially likely to be on public welfare. Since their education has been interrupted, these young mothers usually bring little in the way of skills to the job market. They may also lack adequate child care arrangements. If the mother is a member of a minority group, she may face the additional problem of racial discrimination.

In a survey by Project Redirection, the overwhelming majority of teen mothers interviewed said they would rather work than be on welfare, but they need help in developing marketable skills. (Polit, 7). An example of a successful program is one operated by the YWCA in Salem, Oregon (ibid., 9). This program helps teenage mothers complete work for their high school diploma or GED certificate. The young women receive career education and experience, along with transportation and day care for their children. Getting an education and jobs will enable these young mothers to get off welfare and assume financial independence for themselves and their children.

Special Problems of Single Parents

Single working mothers can have a difficult time balancing their careers, their family responsibilities, and their friends and social life. Many divorced mothers were not employed outside the home before their divorce. Having to find a job, locate appropriate child care, and manage the family budget alone can present traumatic situations for an inexperienced housewife. Even a mother who held a job prior to getting divorced is forced to change her routine when she has the sole responsibility for the children and running the household.

For parents of teenagers and children who are too old for day care, or parents who cannot afford day care, the time between dismissal of school and when the parent comes home from work can be worrisome. Guidelines about such issues as having friends over, chores, and amount and quality of television viewing need to be established, along with procedures for dealing with emergencies, unexpected visitors, and so on. Some communities have programs for teaching children how to handle being home alone. Other communities have hotlines that children may call if they are in trouble, frightened, or just lonely.

Although most single parents are mothers, a growing number of fathers are seeking custody of their children after divorce. The number of single fathers has increased by 127 percent since 1970, and it is anticipated this number will continue to grow (Meredith, 67). Men have started advocacy groups in every state to protest what they consider flagrant judicial bias in favor of mothers, and to encourage more "even-handed" legislation.

Geoffrey Greif has done a study of 1,136 single fathers and found that while about 20 percent of the fathers in the study won custody in court battles, the large majority got their children by consent of the mothers. Most of these mothers believed that the father was a good parent and could offer a more secure home. Greif also reported that fathers are more likely to be awarded older children, even though it is easier for them to rear younger children. The fathers in the study resembled Dustin Hoffman's portrayal of Ted Kramer in *Kramer vs. Kramer*—inept at first in the skills of homemaking, but competent by the end of the movie (Greif, 63).

Fathers who receive custody can have special problems adjusting to balancing job and family. Four out of five fathers in Greif's study said the competing demands were difficult. One result was that the 1,136 fathers in the study experienced 2,158 job changes (ibid.). Fathers who thought of themselves as workers first and fathers second had to shift their values. Many ended up accepting less income and changing their views of themselves by adapting to conflicting demands.

John Moreland, who conducts parenting courses for new single fathers through Ohio State University, says one of the most serious problems these men had was poor communications with their children. Through the use of daily logs in which the fathers recorded the most satisfying interaction with their children and those that were considered problems, the fathers learned about parenting, approaching it much as the mothers did (Meredith, 66).

Sara Bonkowski interviewed an equal number (26 each) of custodial mothers and custodial fathers about their perceptions of the emotional, physical, and social tasks of parents. She found that there was no significant difference between the two groups. Fathers and mothers provided about the same amount of hugs, well-balanced meals, and piano lessons. In many cases, however, the fathers had more money and greater job flexibility, which allowed them to respond more quickly to their children's daily needs (ibid.).

All the studies indicate that a major problem for both single mothers and single fathers is the lack of a satisfying social life. The pain of divorce, diminished income, and the presence of children make it difficult to feel comfortable being single again. The fear of failure in a remarriage can be discouraging, as can children's less-than-positive attitude toward a new partner.

Holidays are often stressful for the single-parent family, with traditions shaken or radically altered. Some parents compensate for the changes in family life by overspending, but love, time together, good food, and a warm house are far more important to feeling good during the holidays. Adding or creating new traditions can help a parent and children feel more like a whole family. The single parent must also save time for him or herself, perhaps sharing a sitter with other families and having time to be alone or do something special.

On the more positive side, one-parent families usually provide fewer direct opportunities for the child to play one parent against the other or to observe inconsistencies in parenting styles. The child only has to please one parent, and some single mothers claim they can devote more time to their children since they do "not have to entertain a mate" (Merritt and Steiner, 160).

Effects on Children of Living in Single-Parent Families

The evidence on the effects on children living in a single-parent family is not conclusive, but some studies indicate trends. Fifty-one percent of the children living in single-parent households headed by their biological mother are in "excellent" health, as are 57 percent living with their biological father and 66 percent living with both biological parents (ibid.). The researchers express caution about these differences, since economic conditions may be the cause of ill health, rather than single-parent family status.

In a study of 64 boys and girls between 6 and 11 years of age, girls who lived with their mothers and boys who lived with their fathers did better on average on the various measures of personality and social development than did children in the custody of opposite-sex parents. "Children with opposite-sex parents tend to be more immature and dependent and to show higher levels of anxiety and lower levels of self-esteem" (Meredith, 67). This study also found indications that children preferred to be with the parent of the same sex. If they were not in same-sex custody arrangements, they wanted more visits with the other parent. The researchers caution, however, that it is important for the child to maintain a relationship with both parents (ibid.).

The issue of role models concerns many single parents, according to Merritt and Steiner. Some single parents emphasized the importance of social gatherings when the family could be around parents of the other sex. Other parents seek pediatricians, babysitters, coaches, or grandparent figures of the opposite sex. Organizations like Big Brothers and Big Sisters can match boys or girls with a same-sex adult, providing special relationships for each of the partners (Merritt and Steiner, 147).

Dornbusch et al. report a reduction in control of adolescents, especially males, in mother-only families. The presence of any other adult in a mother-only household brings control levels closer to those found in two-parent families. This suggests that there are functional equivalents of two-parent families, and that the raising of adolescents is not a task that can easily be handled by a mother alone (Dornbusch et al., 340).

EDUCATIONAL EFFECTS OF LIVING WITH A SINGLE PARENT

Growing up in a single-parent family may take its toll on a child's educational development. Children in single-parent families tend not to get as much schooling as those with two parents at home. In a study of 26-year-olds, researchers found that the men who had lived in female-headed, single-parent families as children had a full year less schooling on average (12.1 compared with 13.1 years) than the national sample as a whole. Among women, those who had lived in a single-parent family also had 12.1 years of education on average, versus 12.5 years for all 26-year-old women ("Upbringing's Toll," 14). Further, children living with only one biological parent are more likely to have repeated a grade in school than children living with both biological parents (Bianchi and Seltzer, 47).

Single parents may have special problems dealing with school-related issues. School teachers and administrators are not always aware of single-parent or divorce situations when they communicate with students' families. Celebrations like father-daughter dinners or mother-son banquets can cause embarrassment for the child living without that parent.

Reflecting the changes in families, many schools now offer parent-child events where the child can bring either parent or even an unrelated but "special" adult. Newsletters and notes are addressed to "parent/guardian" or "family" instead of mom or dad. Conferences are scheduled so that working parents can attend, perhaps even with child care provided for younger children. Some schools offer a sliding scale for fees, events, and special trips for single parents on limited incomes.

Conclusion

The number of single-parent households will continue to increase proportionately. By 1990, half of all children under 18 will have experienced a parental divorce or separation. It is important for our society to know as much as possible about single-parent families and their effects on children, and to find ways to assist single parents and their children to function effectively as families.

REFERENCES

Barney, Joanne, and Judy Koford. "Schools and Single Parents," *The Education Digest* 53, no. 2 (October 1987): 40–43.

Bianchi, Suzanne M., and Judith A. Seltzer. "Life without Father," *American Demographics* 8, no. 12 (December 1986): 43–47.

Danziger, Paula. *The Divorce Express*. New York: Dell, 1982.

Dornbusch, Sanford M., et al. "Single Parents, Extended Households, and the Control of Adolescents," *Child Development* 56, no. 2 (April 1985): 326–341.

Gelman, David, et al. "Playing Both Mother and Father," *Newsweek* 106, no. 3 (15 July 1985): 42–50.

Greif, Geoffrey L. *Single Fathers*. Lexington, MA: D.C. Heath, 1985.

Kantrowitz, Barbara, et al. "Mothers on Their Own," *Newsweek* 106, no. 26 (23 December 1985): 66–67.

Klein, Norma. *Mom, the Wolf Man and Me*. New York: Pantheon, 1972.

Levine, Art, et al. "Taking on Teen Pregnancy," *U.S. News & World Report* 102, no. 11 (23 March 1987): 67–68.

Meredith, Dennis, "Mom, Dad and the Kids: Fathers Going It Alone Are Finding That They, Like Women, Can Rear Children Successfully," *Psychology Today* 19, no. 6 (June 1985): 63–67.

Merritt, Sharyne, and Linda Steiner. *And Baby Makes Two*. New York: Franklin Watts, 1984.

"Mothers Raising Mothers," *U.S. News & World Report* 100, no. 10 (17 March 1986): 24–25.

Polit, Denise F. "Routes to Self-Sufficiency: Teenage Mothers and Employment," *Children Today* 16, no. 1 (January/February 1987): 6–11.

"Upbringing's Toll," *American Demographics* 8, no. 8 (August 1986): 14.

Resources
for Finding Out about Single-Parent Families

Single-Parent Families in Fiction

Adler, C. S. **Down by the River.** New York: Coward, McCann, & Geoghegan, 1981. 206p. Available on cassette.

Having been brought up by a single mother who continues to offer her advice as an adult, Marybeth tells the story of the two men she has loved.

————. **Roadside Valentine.** New York: Macmillan, 1983. 185p.

After Jamie's mother runs off with a Jamaican sea captain and is killed in an auto accident, Jamie and his rigid cardiologist father survive several crises in their relationship and finally come to an understanding.

Ames, Mildred. **Conjuring Summer In.** New York: Harper & Row, 1986. 224p.

In her unhappiness over moving to California, 14-year-old Bernadette experiments with psychic forces. Bizarre characters, a stepbrother, and a single mother create mystery.

Anderson, Mary. **You Can't Get There from Here.** New York: Atheneum, 1982. 194p.

Seventeen-year-old Regina feels abandoned—her father has deserted the family, her mother works and attends evening classes, and her brother is away at college. Regina falls under the influence of a drama teacher who exploits the problems of his students.

Angell, Judie. **What's Best for You: A Novel.** Scarsdale, NY: Bradbury, 1981. 187p.

Three children try to adjust to a new life after their parents divorce. This book probes the emotions of all the family members and shows the parents' willingness to compromise for their children.

Bach, Alice. **A Father Every Few Years.** New York: Harper & Row, 1977. 130p.

When his stepfather leaves home, Tim must cope with his loneliness and learn to deepen his relationships with those still close to him.

Bradbury, Biancha. **In Her Father's Footsteps.** Illustrated by R. Cuffari. Boston: Houghton Mifflin, 1976. 172p.

Eleventh grader Jenny and her widowed father recognize that rebuilding his veterinary hospital will deplete her college fund. Working with her father's fiancée to save some animals helps Jenny learn to like and respect the woman who will become her stepmother.

Branscum, Robbie. **The Saving of P.S.** Illustrated by Glen Rounds. New York: Doubleday, 1977. 127p. Available on cassette for the blind.

A tough stubborn girl from Arkansas who cannot bear to see her father remarry pits all her energies against it. Failing, she runs away and discovers how distorted her ideas and actions have been.

Buchan, Stuart. **When We Lived with Pete.** New York: Scribner, 1978. 147p.

Needing a father, a young boy tries to repair the broken relationship between his widowed mother and her friend Pete.

Butterworth, William Edmund. **Under the Influence.** New York: Four Winds, 1979. 247p.

Two high school seniors, Allan Correli, son of a widowed police chief, and Keith Stevens, son of a widow, meet at football practice and develop a friendship, only to discover their parents are dating. Keith's mother enlists the aid of Mr. Correli in trying to convince her alcoholic son to quit drinking. Keith's drinking leads to tragedy for himself and others.

Byars, Betsy Cromer. **The Animal, the Vegetable and John D. Jones.** New York: Delacorte, 1982. 150p.

Two sisters, on a beach vacation with their father, his woman friend, and her son for two weeks, are sure they are in the wrong place with the wrong people.

————. **The Night Swimmers.** New York: Delacorte, 1980. 144p.

With their mother dead and their father working nights, Retta tries to be mother to her two younger brothers, but somehow things just don't seem to be working out.

Childress, Alice. **A Hero Ain't Nothing But a Sandwich.** New York: Coward, McCann, & Geoghegan, 1973. 126p.

Benjie, who is black, 13 years old, and a heroin addict who denies his addiction, lives with his mother, his grandmother, and his "stepfather," who is not married to his mother.

————. **Rainbow Jordan.** New York: Coward, McCann, & Geoghegan, 1981. 142p.

Rainbow, now 14, is torn by the disparate life-styles of her young, flamboyant, unmarried mother and Miss Josie, the staid, childless, middle-class woman who lets Rainbow live with her.

Clements, Bruce. **Anywhere Else But Here.** New York: Farrar, Straus & Giroux, 1980. 151p.

When her father's printing business goes broke, 13-year-old Molly wants to leave Schenectady, New York, and start over in Connecticut. Two selfish, conniving people complicate matters.

Cohen, Barbara Nash. **The Innkeeper's Daughter.** New York: Lothrop, Lee & Shepard, 1979. 159p.

Although set in the 1940s, this story remains relevant as it depicts 16-year-old Rachel's struggle to deal with her weight problem and unattractiveness. She lives with her attractive, self-assured mother and siblings in the inn that her mother runs.

Colman, Hila. **Weekend Sisters.** New York: Morrow, 1985. 169p.

Fourteen-year-old Amanda sees her father only on weekends. She is upset to learn that he plans to marry a woman with a 16-year-old daughter named Fern. The two girls become rivals for the father's attention, but Fern proves to be untrustworthy and Amanda's father finally apologizes for taking her love for granted.

Conrad, Pam. **Holding Me Here.** New York: Harper & Row, 1986. 184p.

Robin is 14 when her professor father moves out and into an apartment across town. She almost destroys several lives by playing cupid without understanding the undercurrents between separated couples.

Dorman, N. B. **Laughter in the Background.** New York: Elsevier/
Nelson Books, 1980. 158p.

After years of tolerating her divorced mother's alcoholism and
overnight male guests, 12-year-old Marcie finally decides she can
stand it no longer and asks the assistant principal to intercede for her.

Fleagles, Anita Macrae. **The Year the Dreams Came Back.** New York:
Atheneum, 1976. 146p.

For a year after her mother's suicide, teenage Nell tries to suppress
her grief, guilt, and worry. She forms a friendship with Amy, a
woman who runs a bookstore and who later meets and marries
Nell's father.

Fox, Paula. **The Moonlight Man.** New York: Bradbury, 1986. 179p.

Fifteen-year-old Catherine's remarried mother is traveling in Europe,
so she is staying with her long-divorced father. She is frustrated by
his inebriation, but fascinated by his charm.

————. **A Place Apart.** New York: Farrar, Straus & Giroux, 1980.
184p. Available in Braille and on cassette.

After the sudden death of her father, 13-year-old Victoria deals with a
year full of emotional upheavals including reduced family income, a
move from Boston to New Oxford, and her mother's plans to remarry.

Freeman, Gail. **Out from Under.** Scarsdale, NY: Bradbury, 1982. 186p.

After her father dies, a teenage girl must cope with his death, an
uncertain relationship with her mother, the manipulative behavior
of a disturbed friend, and a developing friendship with a boy.

Gerson, Corinne. **How I Put My Mother through College.** New York:
Atheneum, 1981. 136p.

When Jess's newly divorced mother decides to go back to college,
Jess, in a reversal of roles, listens to her ideas and advises her on her
problems.

————. **Son for a Day.** Illustrated by Velma Ilsley. New York:
Atheneum, 1980. 140p.

With his mother on the West Coast and his aunt working nights and
weekends, Danny becomes a helper for single-parent families.

Goldman, Katie. **In the Wings.** New York: Dial, 1982. 166p.

Fifteen-year-old Jessie is thrilled when she gets a major role in the high school play, but dismayed at her parent's divorce and the adjustments to her family's changing relationships.

Greene, Constance Clarke. **I Know You, Al.** Illustrated by B. Barton. New York: Viking, 1975. 126p.

This sequel to *A Girl Called Al*, narrated by her best friend, deals with Al's concern about her divorced mother's boyfriend and her long-absent father's impending marriage. Al learns to accept her father's earlier neglect and his imperfections.

Greene, Sheppard M. **The Boy Who Drank Too Much.** New York: Viking, 1979. 149p.

Narrated by a friend, this story deals with Buff and his single, alcoholic, abusive father. Buff plays on the school hockey team and tries to please his father, an ex-hockey player himself. Buff develops his own drinking problem and finds support in the friendship of peers and an older recovered alcoholic.

Greenwald, Sheila. **Blissful Joy and the SATs: A Multiple Choice Romance.** Boston: Little, Brown, 1982. 143p.

Both of Bliss's divorced parents are involved in new romances, and Bliss realizes that one way out of her chaotic family life is to do well on the SAT exams and get a scholarship to college.

Guernsey, JoAnn Bren. **Journey to Almost There.** New York: Clarion, 1985. 166p.

Alison, 15, runs away from home with her paternal grandfather to search for the artist father who deserted the family when Alison was a baby. Grandfather is suffering from Parkinson's disease and suffers a medical crisis. This and the father's absence from his seedy apartment lead Alison to reconcile with her mother and acknowledge the power of love.

Hayes, Sheila. **Speaking of Snapdragons.** New York: Dutton, 1982. 144p.

Heather befriends an elderly man who gardens, as did the father she can't remember, while her best friend spends the summer trying to adjust to his new stepfather.

Hest, Amy. **Pete and Lily.** New York: Clarion Books, 1986. 120p.

When Pete's widowed mother starts dating Lily's divorced father, the two girls decide they need to control the situation.

Holland, Isabelle. **The Man without a Face.** Philadelphia: Lippincott, 1972. 248p.

Charles, 14, who lives with his two half-sisters and their often-married mother, decides to escape from home by getting into a boarding school. He is tutored by a disfigured recluse and the experience changes his life.

Lyle, Katie Letcher. **Dark but Full of Diamonds.** New York: Coward, McCann, & Geoghegan, 1981. 174p.

A teenager falls in love with the woman his father loves and intends to marry.

Meyer, Carolyn. **Elliott and Win.** New York: Atheneum, 1986. 193p.

After Win and his thrice-divorced mother move to Santa Fe, she registers him in an organization that pairs adult male role models with fatherless boys. Several catastrophic events help Win to see that Elliott is his best friend.

Morgenroth, Barbara. **Will the Real Renie Lake Please Stand Up.** New York: Atheneum, 1981. 164p.

Set in New York, this first-person narrative realistically portrays the struggles of a teenager trying to be her own person amidst the emotional turmoil of her parents' recent divorce.

Myers, Walter Dean. **Motown and Didi.** New York: Viking, 1984. 174p.

Sixteen-year-old Didi is a good student who is seeking a college scholarship as a passport out of Harlem, which she hates. Anger, drugs, and violence are backdrops for Didi and her single, hardworking mother.

Peck, Richard. **Father Figure.** New York: Viking, 1978. 192p.

After their mother's death, 17-year-old Jim and his kid brother Byron go to Florida to live with their father, whom they've never known. Jim experiences feelings of rivalry and resentment toward his father.

————. **Remembering the Good Times.** New York: Delacorte, 1985. 181p.

Kate lives with her grandmother and single mother, and Buck lives with his divorced father. They both become good friends with Trav, an intense, intelligent classmate. Then Trav's suicide disrupts the entire community.

Platt, Kin. **Chloris and the Weirdos.** New York: Bantam, 1980. 231p.

A 13-year-old chronicles life with a mixed-up sister, a twice-divorced mother, and a boyfriend who is an ace skateboarder.

Provost, Gary. **The Pork Chop War.** Scarsdale, NY: Bradbury, 1982. 192p.

Brian and his brothers fight over everything until a young man who seems more like another kid than a father figure joins the family.

Rodowsky, Colby F. H. **My Name is Henley.** New York: Farrar, Straus & Giroux, 1982. 184p.

Henley follows her mother from place to place until she finds one that she refuses to leave.

Sebestyen, Ouida. **Far from Home.** Boston: Little, Brown, 1980. 191p.

After the death of his mute, unmarried mother, 13-year-old Salty goes with his grandmother to work in the Buckley Arms Hotel where he learns about love and family.

———. **IOU's.** Boston: Little, Brown, 1982. 188p.

Living with his divorced mother, 13-year-old Stowe Garrett is caught between the loyalty he feels for her and a yearning to know his relatives and to break free.

Simons, Wendy. **Harper's Mother.** Englewood Cliffs, NJ: Prentice-Hall, 1980. 220p.

Once again, Harper and her mother leave the man with whom they've been living and look for a new situation.

Slote, Alfred. **Love and Tennis.** New York: Macmillan, 1979. 163p.

Fifteen-year-old Buddy Berger's divorced mother is also his tennis coach. When Buddy beats a nationally ranked player in a local tennis tournament, she decides it is time for him to begin developing his talent in earnest. Buddy has two dilemmas: judging whether his athletic talent obligates him to be ruthlessly competitive, and trying to remain loyal to both of his parents.

Strang, Celia. **This Child Is Mine.** New York: Beaufort, 1981. 156p.

A 14-year-old assumes the role of mother for her unmarried sister's baby in a poor family afflicted with numerous problems.

Voigt, Cynthia. **A Solitary Blue.** New York: Atheneum, 1983. 189p.

Jeff Green's mother left home when he was seven, and his professor father is too self-engrossed to be aware of Jeff's feelings of abandonment. But his father helps when Jeff's mother betrays him yet again.

Nonfiction Materials on Single-Parent Families

BOOKS

Capaldi, Fredrick, and Barbara McRae. **Stepfamilies: A Cooperative Responsibility.** New York: Franklin Watts, 1979.

Chapter 3, "The Single-Parent Family," discusses the single mother, the single father, the absentee parent, and the concerns of children in the aftermath of divorce and a changed family structure.

Croner, Helga B., compiler. **National Directory of Private Social Agencies.** Queens Village, NY: Croner Publications, 1988.

A directory of private social agencies in the United States designed for persons in the "helping professions" and those in need of help. Services to single parents are included as a category.

Dolmetsch, Paul, and Alexa Shis, editors. **The Kids' Book about Single-Parent Families: Kids for Everyone.** Garden City, NY: Doubleday, 1985. 193p.

Children describe their experiences and problems living with a single parent, including unmarried mothers, divorced parents, and parents whose spouses have died.

Duncan, Barbara. **Single Mother's Survival Manual.** Saratoga, CA: R & E Publishers, 1984. 172p.

The author discusses strategies for surviving single-parenting, including "enlightened selfishness," employment, living within your means, and the legal aspects of being single.

Gilbert, Sara. **How To Live with a Single Parent.** New York: Lothrop, Lee & Shepard, 1981. 128p.

In this book for middle school students, the author talks about feelings when parents split, and the causes of conflict from dating, remarriage, and money. She includes a list of children's organizations and addresses as well as a list for parents.

Greif, Geoffrey L. **Single Fathers.** Lexington, MA: D. C. Heath, 1985. 194p.

Based on the survey responses of more than 1,100 fathers raising children alone after separation or divorce, this book offers single fathers support while painting an accurate picture of their day-to-day struggles and achievements. One section involves relationships with an ex-wife, and another discusses the special problems fathers face from the legal system.

Hall, Nancy Lee. **The True Story of a Single Mother.** Boston: South End Press, 1984. 185p.

The personal story of the author's survival through the emotional conflicts, disappointments, and joys of single parenting, including attending her ex-husband's second wedding.

Horner, Catherine Townsend. **The Single-Parent Family in Children's Books: An Annotated Bibliography.** Metuchen, NJ: Scarecrow, 1988. 172p.

Annotations are included for 215 titles that span 100 years of children's fiction portraying one-parent families. The books are divided into the causes for single-parent status, including divorce, unwed mothers, orphans, widows, and protracted absence of one parent. Some nonfiction books are also included. The indexes list entries by title, author, and subject.

Keshet, Jamie Kelem. **Love and Power in the Stepfamily.** New York: McGraw-Hill, 1987. 231p.

Chapter 3, "Parenting after Divorce," suggests ways the "mini-family" can deal with childrearing activities in two separate households. Each parent becomes a generalist in the household rather than a specialist, and children adjust to their own changing roles and to those of their parents.

Lee, Laurel. **Mourning into Dancing.** New York: Dutton, 1984. 218p.

After her battle with Hodgkin's disease (described in an earlier book) the author remarries, only to have this marriage end in divorce also. She learns to live as a single parent of three children.

McCoy, Kathleen. **Solo Parenting: Your Essential Guide: How To Find the Balance between Parenthood and Personhood.** New York: New American Library, 1987. 269p.

Through stories, interviews, and talks with professionals, the author has developed strategies for loving child care and effective self-care. She discusses overcoming guilt, easing the transition from a two-parent to a single-parent family, and managing money. The appendix includes organizations to assist solo parents.

Miner, Jane Claypool. **Young Parents.** Photographs by Maureen McNicholas. New York: Messner, 1985. 159p.

Miner discusses the choices open to adolescent girls who become pregnant and the consequences of their decisions. A wide range of topics includes money, "bonding," isolation from peers, and the teen's relationship with her parents and with the child's father.

Murdock, Carol Vejvoda. **Single Parents Are People, Too: How To Achieve a Positive Self-Image and Personal Satisfaction.** New York: Butterick, 1980. 192p.

The strong message of this book is that single parents are a worthwhile segment of each community, and they need social support. The author relates many personal narratives based on information gathered through interviews and questionnaires.

Rowlands, Peter. **Saturday Parent: A Book for Separated Families.** New York: Continuum, 1982. 143p.

This is a book for the other parent, the one who lives apart from his or her children and sees them only occasionally. The author interviewed many "Saturday parents" and their children to get firsthand information, and concluded it is important and worthwhile for parents to stay in touch with their children even though they no longer live together.

Sadler, Judith DeBoard. **Families in Transition: An Annotated Bibliography.** Hamden, CT: Archon Books, 1988. 251p.

A bibliography on family life in the United States, with sections on the single-parent family, stepfamilies, and unmarried couples.

Schlesinger, Benjamin. **The One-Parent Family in the 1980s: Perspectives and Annotated Bibliography, 1978–1984.** Toronto: University of Toronto Press, 1985. 284p.

The contents include such chapters as "Custodial Parents: Review and a Longitudinal Study," "Single Fathers with Custody," and "The

Single Teen-Age Canadian Mother in the 1980s." The annotated bibliography has sections addressing children in one-parent families, treatment and services for one-parent families, female-headed and male-headed one-parent families, widows and widowers heading one-parent families, and nonmarried parents.

Worth, Richard. **The American Family.** Photographs by Robert Sefcik. New York: Franklin Watts, 1984. 120p.

The author analyzes the role of the family in society and examines different types of families, including single-parent families, unmarried couples living together, and the traditional nuclear family.

ARTICLES

Barney, Joanne, and Judy Koford. **"Schools and Single Parents,"** *The Education Digest* 53, no. 2 (October 1987): 40–43.

Suggestions for ways teachers and schools can be more helpful to single parents and noncustodial parents who are concerned about their children's success in school.

Bianchi, Suzanne M., and Judith A. Seltzer. **"Life without Father,"** *American Demographics* 8, no. 12 (December 1986): 43–47.

The authors see the stereotypical image of families changing and relate the changes to health, money, and psychological aspects.

"Children Who Get Cut Out," *U.S. News & World Report* 103, no. 15 (12 October 1986): 24–25.

All 50 states have passed laws to garnishee paychecks of fathers who abandon families, but often the law doesn't translate into money for single parents.

Dornbusch, Sanford M., et al. **"Single Parents, Extended Households, and the Control of Adolescents,"** *Child Development* 56, no. 2 (April 1985): 326–341.

Using a representative national sample of adolescents to study the interrelationships among family structure, patterns of family decision making, and deviant behavior in adolescents, the authors show mother-only households appear to have reduced control of adolescents.

Gallman, Vanessa. **"Holidays and Single Moms,"** *Essence* 18, no. 8 (December 1987): 102p.

The article gives concrete suggestions to help single mothers cope with holidays in general and Christmas in particular, including spending special time with the children, avoiding overspending, and saving time for oneself.

Gelman, David, et al. **"Playing Both Mother and Father,"** *Newsweek* 106, no. 3 (15 July 1985): 42–43.

With one out of four households with children headed by a single parent and the number expected to double by 1990, the authors share financial and psychological burdens discovered.

―――. **"The Single Parent: Family Albums,"** *Newsweek* 106, no. 3 (15 July 1985): 44–50

Putting the stories of five families in the context of society's expectations, the authors include specifics about money and social life. They conclude that many children of single-parent homes become mature, responsible, happy adults.

Kantrowitz, Barbara. **"Mothers on Their Own,"** *Newsweek* 106, no. 26 (23 December 1985): 66–67.

Formed in 1981, Single Mothers by Choice is a group of women who want babies, with or without husbands. The group now has more than 1,000 members.

Levine, Art, et al. **"Taking on Teen Pregnancy,"** *U.S. News & World Report* 102, no. 11 (23 March 1987) 67–68.

Since many teen pregnancies result in single-parent families with low incomes, schools and other organizations are concerned with plans to prevent teen pregnancy.

McCall, Robert B. **"When Fathers Have Custody,"** *Parents* 62, no. 8 (August 1987): 211.

Admitting that fathers generally have higher incomes, McCall points out the strengths and weaknesses of fathers as the heads of single-parent households.

Meredith, Dennis. **"Mom, Dad and the Kids: Fathers Going It Alone Are Finding That They, Like Women, Can Rear Children Successfully,"** *Psychology Today* 19, no. 6 (June 1985): 63–67.

Using both study results and specific examples from the lives of men who have succeeded at homemaking and careers simultaneously, the author shows there is no difference between men and women as primary caretakers of children.

"Mothers Raising Mothers," *U.S. News & World Report* 100, no. 10 (17 March 1986): 24–25.

The article reports that 80 to 90 percent of births to black teenagers in some cities were out of wedlock.

Polit, Denise F. **"Routes to Self-Sufficiency: Teenage Mothers and Employment,"** *Children Today* 16, no. 1 (January/February 1987): 6–11.

Unmarried teenage mothers are the focus of this article, which emphasizes programs that offer them vocational and employment-related services.

"Upbringing's Toll," *American Demographics* 8, no. 8 (August 1986): 14.

A comparative study of 26-year-olds from female-headed, single-parent families and those from two-parent families found that subjects raised in single-parent families averaged a full year less of school for males and a half-year less for females than their counterparts from two-parent homes.

Walton, Susan. **"Single-Parent Families: New Script, Same Action,"** *Psychology Today* 19, no. 3 (March 1985): 79.

Although the author expected single-parent families to reflect less stereotypical attitudes about sex roles than two-parent families, she found single-parent families were no less traditional about tasks and toys for girls and boys.

Nonprint Materials on Single-Parent Families

Backtrack

Type:	Various video formats
Length:	14 min.
Cost:	Purchase, no amount indicated
Distributor:	Phoenix Films & Video
	468 Park Avenue South
	New York, NY 10016
Date:	1977

A drifter, 15 years on the road, meets up with his 15-year-old daughter and the child's mother in this program, the theme of which is responsibility.

Dads and Kids

Type:	¹/₂″ video
Length:	28 min.
Cost:	Rental $12
Distributor:	Beacon Films
	930 Pitner Avenue
	Evanston, IL 60202
Date:	1985

Through candid interviews with five single fathers and their children, this program communicates the joys and frustrations of being the primary parent and the kinds of adjustments parents face after the breakup of a marriage.

Hard Times

Type:	16mm film or video
Length:	29 min.
Cost:	Purchase $395 (film), $245 (video)
Distributor:	Instructional Television Library
	P.O. Box 80669
	Lincoln, NE 68501
Date:	1982

A teenage mother attempts to survive the strains of single parenthood alone. Only when she accepts help is she able to gain control of her life.

It's Just Better

Type:	16mm film or video
Length:	15 min.
Cost:	Rental $40, purchase $350 (film); rental $40, purchase $250 (video)
Distributor:	National Film Board of Canada
	1251 Avenue of the Americas, 16th Floor
	New York, NY 10020
Date:	1982

A young country boy with nine siblings and a single parent talks about his father's drinking problem, making ends meet, and being part of a large household where cooperation is crucial.

Izzy

Type:	16mm film or video
Length:	42 min.
Cost:	Rental $50, purchase $595 (film); rental $50, purchase $225 (video)

Distributor: Media Guild
                 11722 Sorrento Valley Road, Suite E
                 San Diego, CA 92121
Date: 1985

This film explores the problems faced by the child of a mixed race marriage growing up in a single parent family. The film emphasizes parent-child relationships.

The Kreinik and Bosworth Families: Single Adoptive Parents
Type: 16mm film or video
Length: 7 min.
Cost: Rental $35, purchase $170 (film); rental $35, purchase
                 $85 (video)
Distributor: Films Inc.
                 5547 N. Ravenswood Avenue
                 Chicago, IL 60640-1199
Date: 1979

Two single parents, one male and one female, discuss their choices to adopt children and the problems and benefits they found. From the series The American Family: An Endangered Species.

One of a Kind
Type: 16mm film or video
Length: 58 min.
Cost: Rental $65, purchase $795 (film); rental $65, purchase
                 $495 (video)
Distributor: Phoenix Films & Video Inc.
                 468 Park Avenue South
                 New York, NY 10016
Date: 1978

A divorced mother overcome with life's problems begins beating her daughter.

Peggy Collins: Single Mother
Type: 16mm film or video
Length: 9 min.
Cost: Rental $35, purchase $195 (film); rental $35, purchase
                 $100 (video)
Distributor: Films Inc.
                 5547 N. Ravenswood Avenue
                 Chicago, IL 60640-1199
Date: 1979

A divorced waitress struggles to make ends meet and to cope with her daughter's adjustment to their new way of life. The program looks at personal, social, and economic effects of divorce. From the series The American Family: An Endangered Species.

Raising Michael Alone

Type:	16mm film
Length:	17 min.
Cost:	Rental $40, purchase $310
Distributor:	Educational Development Center
	39 Chapel Street
	Newton, MA 02160
Date:	1977

The single mother of an 11-year-old boy discusses raising her child by herself.

Sean's Story: Divided Custody

Type:	16mm film or video
Length:	12 min.
Cost:	Rental $40, purchase $245 (film); rental $40, purchase $125 (video)
Distributor:	Films Inc.
	5547 N. Ravenswood Avenue
	Chicago, IL 60640-1199
Date:	1979

Although they live in different parts of the United States, Sean's parents have joint custody and take turns bringing him up. A grandparent gives Sean a sense of his origins and his family ties. From the series The American Family: An Endangered Species.

Single Fathering

Type:	16mm film
Length:	8 min.
Cost:	Rental $50, purchase $200
Distributor:	Ron Taylor
	1502 Columbine
	Boulder, CO 80302
Date:	1982

An unmarried man with an adopted child explains his decision to be a single parent.

Single Parent

Type:	16mm film or video
Length:	40 min.

Cost: Rental $50, purchase $585 (film); rental $50, purchase
                   $410 (video)
Distributor: Media Guild
                   11722 Sorrento Valley Road, Suite E
                   San Diego, CA 92121
Date: 1976

Common misconceptions about single parenting are exposed as this
film looks at the day-to-day life of a divorced mother.

Single Parent Family
Type: 16mm color film
Length: 15 min.
Cost: Rental $11.50
Distributor: Centron Films
                   108 Wilmot Road
                   Deerfield, IL 60015-9990
Date: 1981

After her divorce, Helene struggles to adjust to raising her children
with limited financial support. She meets Ray at a Parents Without
Partners meeting. From the series Family Life: Transitions in Marriage
(A Case History).

The Single Parent Family
Type: 16mm film or video
Length: 15 min.
Cost: Rental $40, purchase $335 (film); rental $40, purchase
                   $235 (video)
Distributor: Coronet Film and Video
                   108 Wilmot Road
                   Deerfield, IL 60015-9990
Date: 1981

This case study brings up issues relevant to single parents. From the
series Family Life: Transitions in Marriage.

Single Parenting: Crisis and Challenge
Type: 16mm film
Length: 29 min.
Cost: Rental $35
Distributor: Parents Without Partners
                   7910 Woodmont Avenue
                   Washington, DC 20014
Date: 1980

Four families adjusting to new lives with single parents reveal the potential for positive change as they adapt to bereavement, separation, and divorce.

Single Parents

Type:	16mm film or video
Length:	29 min.
Cost:	Rental $65, purchase $450 (film); rental $50, purchase $300 (video)
Distributor:	Martha Stuart Communications 147 W. 22nd Street New York, NY 10011
Date:	1980

Single parents of both sexes talk about responsibilities and benefits of raising children without partners. From the series Are You Listening?

Single Parents and Other Adults

Type:	16mm film or video
Length:	25 min.
Cost:	Rental $60, purchase $475 (film); rental $60, purchase $335 (video)
Distributor:	MTI Teleprograms Inc. 108 Wilmot Road Deerfield, IL 60015-9990
Date:	1982

This film addresses common problems for recently divorced parents, such as emotional trauma, visitation rights, budgets, and dating.

Single Parents and Their Children

Type:	16mm film or video
Length:	18 min.
Cost:	Rental $60, purchase $350 (film); rental $60, purchase $245 (video)
Distributor:	MTI Teleprograms Inc. 108 Wilmot Road Deerfield, IL 60015-9990
Date:	1982

Through dramatizations about single parents, this film raises issues of visitation rights, meeting new people, emotional problems, and living arrangements.

Single-Parent Families: Coping with Change

Type:	Filmstrip or video
Length:	18 min.
Cost:	Purchase $32
Distributor:	McGraw-Hill
	Education Resources
	P.O. Box 408
	Hight's Town, NJ 08520
Date:	1987

This work gives an overview of both the problems and the positive aspects of single-parent households through a portrayal of three fictional families, each headed by one adult.

Teen Mother: A Story of Coping

Type:	16mm film or video
Length:	24 min.
Cost:	Purchase $440 (film), $350 (video)
Distributor:	Churchill Films
	662 N. Robertson Boulevard
	Los Angeles, CA 90069
Date:	1981

Vignettes based on Rosie, an actual teenage mother, who decides to go on welfare and join a support group as ways of coping with adolescent parenthood.

Organizations Concerned with Single-Parent Families

Big Brothers, Big Sisters of America
230 N. 13th Street
Philadelphia, PA 19107
(215) 567-7000
Executive Director: Thomas McKenna

The national organization provides standards and procedures for 460 local agencies, which are supervised by field representatives. The organization assists single parents who wish to provide opposite sex-role models for their children; for instance, a male role model for a child of a single mother. The local agencies have some flexibility in how they implement their procedures, so readers should check their telephone directory to learn about the organization in their locality.

The telephone number given above may be used for referral from the national office to a local agency.

Parents Without Partners
8807 Colesville Road
Silver Spring, MD 20910
(301) 588-9354
International President: Richard Stewart

Founded in 1957, this national group has local chapters that help single custodial and noncustodial parents and their children. The parent may be single through widowhood, divorce, separation, or otherwise. The organization promotes research and study, legislation, and public affairs for its members, and is a source of information and referrals for single parents.

PUBLICATIONS: *The Single Parent* (bimonthly), plus bibliographies, manuals, resource list, and brochures.

Single Mothers by Choice
P.O. Box 1642
Gracie Square Station
New York, NY 10028
(212) 988-0993
Chairperson: Jane Mattes

Formed in 1981, this organization provides information and support for more than 1,000 members across the United States. Members are primarily single professional women in their 30s and 40s who have either decided to or are considering bearing or adopting children outside of marriage as single parents.

PUBLICATION: *SMC Newsletter* (20/year).

Single Parent Resource Center
1165 Broadway, Room 504
New York, NY 10001
(212) 213-0047

The center was founded in 1981 to establish a network of local single parent groups in order to give such groups a collective political voice.

Sisterhood of Black Single Mothers
1360 Fulton Street, Suite 423
Brooklyn, NY 11216

(718) 638-0413
Executive Director: Daphne Busby

Founded in 1973 for black single mothers, including widows and women who are divorced, separated, or have never been married, the organization's purpose is to develop a positive self-image in members and to act as a referral service to assist members in contacting aid-giving institutions and individuals. Although concentrated in New York City, the group's membership is nationwide.

PUBLICATION: Newsletter (quarterly).

CHAPTER 4

Grandparents and Other Relatives

Polly always made us put up a card table. It was handier for her wheelchair, and she took her game playing seriously. . . . she taught us some card games, "real games," in her opinion: crazy eights, spit in the ocean, all played by her rules. Polly was a demon at cards, playing for blood and sneaking peeks at our hands. She was about bald, and the ceiling light gleamed on the dome of her scalp. All she lacked was a green eyeshade.

Richard Peck, *Remembering the Good Times*
(New York: Dell, 1985), 30–31.

Kate's mom has a job and goes out a lot at night, so Kate takes care of Polly, her great-grandmother. Polly's wit and insight make her the center of many of the activities of the young people in Peck's book.

Before our society became so mobile, parents and grandparents lived much closer together, sometimes in the same house. In these extended family networks, grandparents took an active role in the nurturing of the young (Kornhaber and Woodward, xxvii). There are societies where such arrangements are still common, but in the United States, extended family members have much less contact with one another than in the past.

The relationships between grandchildren and grandparents, as well as between other individuals involved in the extended family, will be the focus of this chapter.

Terms

Extended family. Relatives or other individuals who are accepted into the family, sharing responsibility and caring for each other.

Multigenerational household. A term used by social scientists to indicate a family where grandparents or other older relatives cohabitate with their grandchildren and children (ibid.).

Research on Grandparents and Grandchildren

Realizing that few researchers had examined the relationship between grandparents and grandchildren, Arthur Kornhaber and Kenneth L. Woodward interviewed 300 grandparents and 300 grandchildren, including only an occasional related pair. Their research is summarized in the book *Grandparents/Grandchildren: The Vital Connection*:

- Of the children in the study, only 5 percent had a warm relationship with one or more grandparents (Kornhaber and Woodward, 37).
- About 80 percent of the children felt removed or polarized from their grandparents, having sporadic and not always happy connections with them (ibid., 41).
- About 15 percent of the children had never experienced any attachment to a grandparent (ibid., 42).

Kornhaber and Woodward believe that although a limited number of children in their sample had close ties with grandparents, families can recover these natural, intergenerational ties. They concluded that regardless of how grandparents act, they affect the emotional well-being of their grandchildren, for better or worse, simply because they exist.

The 5 percent of children who had warm relationships with grandparents considered themselves "lucky." When they talked about their grandparents, these children remembered what they did with them, how they smelled, and their personal quirks and foibles. They rarely mentioned gifts from grandparents, unless they were heirlooms.

The majority of the children in the study indicated their grandparents had receded into the background of their lives, yet were in the foreground of their emotional concerns. They felt attached to grandparents who were physically and/or emotionally separated from them. The most distressed children were those who were physically near but emotionally distant from grandparents. They resented having to give "command performances" of affection and were keenly aware of a generation gap.

The remaining group of children, about 15 percent, had never experienced any attachment to a grandparent, but appeared anxious to learn about grandparents. They built their expectations on the portrayals of grandparents in books, movies, and television programs, many of which are stereotypes.

The Roles of Grandparents Today

SOURCES OF HISTORICAL KNOWLEDGE

Grandparents are a source of information of previous times, unwritten stories about children's parents, and events in the family history. Such knowledge provides "generational continuity" (Kornhaber, 12) and a sense of family cohesiveness. One grandparent from the Kornhaber study had made a "family museum" in his attic, where his grandchildren could experience a connection with their family's past through preserved love letters, toys, and clothes.

Nearly all children are interested in what other generations did when they were young and what it was like before contemporary conveniences. Some grandparents write or tape accounts of family history, often accompanied by decades of family photos. Such histories can include anecdotes about family members, accounts of significant events they may have witnessed, and descriptions of life at school, work, or home. Sometimes younger members "interview" older relatives to gather such information, recording the interview on audio or video tape or making a written account. Many families are now recording current events on videotape, so that future grandchildren may be able to witness their family histories in vivid detail.

Family skills and secrets are also passed on from grandparents to grandchild. Whether it is a family recipe for soup or jam, a hint on how to succeed in some particular enterprise, or the secrets of successful flycasting for fish, grandparents have a lifetime of experience to share with young people. Other lessons include ethics, morals, and behavior that children may not learn anywhere else. All these are learned in a nonpressured atmosphere of loving acceptance and unconditional love (ibid.).

NURTURERS AND FRIENDS

Parents may feel secure in the knowledge that grandparents are available for counseling, caring for the children, and financial and emotional support for the family. Most parents want to feel independent, and most grandparents want to be asked for their views. But pride of each generation should not get in the way of sharing, which is beneficial for all parties involved.

Grandparents and grandchildren often plot together against the middle generation, the parents. Grandparents can be persuaded to go places parents won't go and to buy things parents won't buy. They can also be confidants for hopes, dreams and misdeeds that parents might misunderstand or be upset by. That the plots are often known by the parents doesn't lessen the pleasure of the game. Mature parents, rather than feeling left out of the fun, understand the conspiracy and look the other way (ibid., 13).

The love and respect between grandchildren and grandparents also affects the way children regard and treat other old people in the society. Kornhaber cites an example of a street-hardened 18-year-old who said he couldn't take an old lady's purse because she reminded him of his grandmother. It was after his grandmother died that this boy started getting into trouble (ibid., 14).

Grandparents and Their Divorced Children

The prevalence of divorce in today's society means that many grandparents will experience drastic changes in their family structure. In cases where the divorce is bitter, grandparents on the noncustodial side of the family may find their access to grandchildren abruptly cut off. In most states, grandparents have no legal rights to see their grandchildren, although a number of grandparents are suing for visitation rights around the country. The possibility of not seeing one another again adds to the trauma of divorce for both grandparents and grandchildren.

On the plus side, grandparents may serve as a source of emotional and even financial support during and after the divorce. They may provide child care for new single parents, as well as a sense of continuity and continued security for the children. Because grandparents have maturity and more experience, they can bring judgment and a mellowed approach to the situation. Divorce is difficult for everyone involved, but grandparents can be a definite asset to the entire family.

When Grandparents Divorce

Divorce is not something that happens just in young families. With more people living longer, the possibility exists that more divorces will occur among older people. Such a situation can create difficult adjustments for the children and the grandchildren, including visiting two locations to see grandparents, adapting to new life-styles of the grandparents, and vicariously experiencing the pain of separation and divorce. If one or both of the grandparents remarry, everyone has to adjust to those new relationships as well.

Illness and Death of Grandparents

Young people often have their first experience with serious illness and death through their grandparents. The death of a grandparent may be a child's or adolescent's first experience with grief. Serious illnesses such as cancer, strokes, or Alzheimer's disease may alter the grandparent's appearance or personality beyond recognition. When health problems make it difficult for grandparents to take care of themselves, they or family members may decide that they need to be in a retirement center or a nursing home. Such decisions may cause painful and difficult adjustments for all family members.

Other Extended Family Members

Although this chapter has focused on grandparents, other relatives may live with the family or play important roles in children's development. These other relatives can be uncles, aunts, or cousins. Because they share the family's history, they may find a comfortable place in the household and provide continuity in the family.

When grandparents and other relatives are not nearby, parents may seek compatible neighbors or friends to join the family for celebrations, birthdays, or other special occasions. Many people have "extended families" made up of unrelated individuals who provide the support and closeness that used to come from relatives. The presence of such adults provides children and teenagers with an appreciation of their elders' points of view and helps them maintain contact with people outside their own generation.

REFERENCES

Kornhaber, Arthur. *Between Parents and Grandparents.* New York: St. Martin's Press, 1986.

Kornhaber, Arthur, and Kenneth L. Woodward. *Grandparents/Grandchildren: The Vital Connection.* New Brunswick, NJ: Transaction Books, 1985.

Peck, Richard. *Remembering the Good Times.* New York: Dell, 1985.

Resources
for Finding Out about Relatives and Extended Families

Relatives and Extended Families in Fiction

Adler, C. S. **The Shell Lady's Daughter.** New York: Coward-McCann, 1983. 119p.

When Kelly's mother has to be hospitalized for mental illness, Kelly is taken to her grandparents' home on a Florida beach. From observing Grandmother's courage and her attentiveness to Kelly's ill, uncommunicative grandfather, the girl learns what love and caring are about.

Bach, Alice. **Mollie Make-Believe.** New York: Dell, 1976. 160p.

Events take place in the apartment of Mollie's dying grandmother, where Mollie experiences the pain of growing up, becoming independent, and the death of a loved one.

Bess, Clayton. **Big Man and the Burn-Out.** Boston: Houghton Mifflin, 1985. 208p.

Jess has lived with his grandparents since his mother deserted him when he was a baby. In this story he learns some important lessons in nurturing and finally smooths some of the tensions that have existed between him and his grandmother.

Brancato, Robin. **Sweet Bells Jangled Out of Tune.** New York: Knopf, 1982. 200p.

Ellen Dohrmann realizes she and her mother no longer visit her deceased father's mother, Grandma Eva, who has become an eccentric bag lady in their town. Investigating the situation, Ellen sees that Eva needs help and tries to make up for past neglect.

Bridgers, Sue Ellen. **All Together Now.** New York: Knopf, 1979. 256p.

This novel depicts Casey Flanagan's coming-of-age during the summer she lives in her grandmother's small hometown, while her father is in Korea and her mother works two jobs.

————. **Notes for Another Life.** New York: Knopf, 1981. 250p.

Because their father is mentally ill and their mother decides on a career that takes her to the city, Kevin and Wren live with their grandparents. The story is a wonderful portrayal of their active grandmother who plays tennis, cooks, shows concern, and knows the right things to say to people.

————. **Permanent Connections.** New York: Harper & Row, 1987. 264p.

Rob, an angry teenager who is always on the edge of trouble, is sent to help out on the old family farm in southern Appalachia. He hates the place and keeps himself apart from the troubled relatives he barely knows. They all struggle with the connections of their lives.

Carillo, Charles. **Shepherd Avenue.** Boston: Atlantic Monthly Press, 1986. 299p.

After his mother's death, a shy ten-year-old boy must find a place for himself in his grandparents' boisterous Italian family in New York City.

Corcoran, Barbara. **Hey, That's My Soul You're Stomping On!** New York: Atheneum, 1978. 144p.

Rachel, visiting her grandparents in Palm Springs, learns to love both them and the town while her parents debate and finally seek a divorce.

Dixon, Paige. **Skipper.** New York: Atheneum, 1979. 110p.

Teenage Skipper Phillips' journey to North Carolina to visit the family of the father he's never known helps him overcome his confusion and sense of loss after his brother's death. He discovers an entire clan of Phillipses, including a spoiled half-brother, a great-grandfather, and cousins, as well as his father.

Dorris, Michael. **A Yellow Raft in Blue Water.** New York: H. Holt, 1987. 343p.

Contemporary American Indian women representing three generations tell their stories: 15-year-old Rayona longs for a suburban family life, but her mother abandons her on the barren Montana reservation with her fierce grandmother who doesn't know her and doesn't want to.

Farber, Norma. **How Does It Feel To Be Old?** Illustrated by Trina Schart Hyman. New York: Dutton, 1979. 28p.
A grandmother tells her visiting granddaughter what it is like to be old. She recognizes both the good (being free of parental advice) and the bad (treats don't taste as good as they used to).

Garcia, Ann O'Neal. **Spirit on the Wall.** New York: Holiday House, 1982. 192p.
Set in Cro-Magnon times, this is the story of Em, who is born with a crooked leg and would have been killed because of her deformity were it not for her grandmother, who rescues her and raises her to be independent and self-sufficient.

Hamilton, Virginia. **A Little Love.** New York: Philomel Books, 1984. 207p.
A black teenager, who has been raised lovingly by her grandparents, goes in search of her father.

Howker, Janni. **The Nature of the Beast.** New York: Greenwillow, 1985. 137p.
A boy, his father, and his grandfather try to care for each other in harsh times.

Hunt, Irene. **Up a Road Slowly.** Chicago: Follett, 1966. 192p. Available as a Talking Book.
This Newbery Award winner deals with a girl's maturation from 7 to 17 and her response to and growing love for her aunt. After the death of her mother, she chooses to live with her aunt and uncle instead of her father and his new wife.

Irwin, Hadley. **What about Grandma?** New York: Atheneum, 1982. 165p.
Sixteen-year-old Rhys is caught in the middle between her stubborn mother and her strong-willed grandmother. The first-person account by Rhys and reflections on aging enrich this book.

Kaye, Geraldine. **Comfort Herself.** Andre Deutsch, 1985; distributed by Dutton, New York. 160p.

When her mother dies, Comfort, a child of mixed race, is faced with a difficult choice: whether to remain in England with her English grandmother or to make a new home in Ghana, where her paternal grandmother has taken a liking to her.

Lyon, George Ella. **Borrowed Children.** New York: Watts/Orchard, 1988. 154p.
Twelve-year-old Amanda narrates this subtly characterized intergenerational family story set in Depression-era Kentucky and Tennessee.

Maguire, Gregory. **The Lightning Time.** New York: Farrar, Straus & Giroux, 1978. 256p.
In this well-wrought fantasy, 12-year-old Daniel is sent to visit a grandmother he has never seen. He discovers that she is a likable old lady and becomes involved in a fight to stop a greedy developer from taking over the unspoiled mountain she owns.

Mazer, Norma Fox. **A Figure of Speech.** New York: Dell, 1973. 159 pp.
Jenny is especially close to her grandfather, who has lived in her family's basement apartment since she was born. When her brother brings home a bride, Grandpa is pushed out of his place and shoved towards an old folks' home, but he and Jenny take matters into their own hands.

Mearian, Judy Frank. **Someone Slightly Different.** New York: Dial, 1980. 197p.
Marty's grandmother, who drinks a little and bets on the horses, provides a warmth that his cab-driving, divorced mother isn't able to.

Miles, Miska. **Annie and the Old One.** Illustrated by Peter Parnall. Boston: Little, Brown, 1971. 44p.
Annie is a little Navajo girl whose grandmother is special to her. Grandmother says that when the new rug she is weaving is finished, she will die. Annie plots ways to keep the rug from being finished. Although this is a picture book, it has appeal for all ages.

Peck, Richard. **Remembering the Good Times.** New York: Dell, 1985. 181p.
Kate, who lives with her great-grandmother Polly; Buck, who lives with his divorced father; and Trav, who comes from an affluent home, form a close friendship during their high school years. Polly serves as a stabilizing influence on all of them.

Porter, Barbara Ann. **I Only Made Up the Roses.** New York: Greenwillow, 1987. 114p.

Cydra is part of a dynamic extended family, and stories from both her black and her white relatives are woven into her identity.

Ruby, Lois. **Two Truths in My Pocket.** New York: Viking, 1982. 137p.

Six short stories about Jewish teenagers present a variety of characters and settings. "Frail Bridge" is about 16-year-old Rochela whose great-grandmother has died. Her memories of the disagreeable aspects of the nursing home are haunting, but she is finally able to come to terms with the situation and mourn her loss.

Shyer, Marlene Fanta. **Grandpa Ritz and the Luscious Lovelies.** New York: Scribner, 1985. 170p.

Philip spends a summer with his grandfather to help him adjust to living alone in a retirement community and finds it more of an adventure than he expected.

Thomas, Karen. **Changing of the Guard.** New York: Harper & Row, 1986. 186p.

Sixteen-year-old Caroline is devastated by the death of her beloved grandfather and spends her time with her elderly grandmother or alone until a flamboyant new girl at school befriends her.

Tolan, Stephanie S. **Grandpa—and Me.** New York: Scribner's, 1978. 120p.

Kerry, nearly 12, tape records the story as she begins to see Grandpa, who has lived with her family since Kerry was three, suddenly behaving strangely. She realizes that none of the family has been paying attention to him, and her summer becomes quite different because of this.

Vallo, Lawrence Jonathan. **Tales of a Pueblo Boy.** Santa Fe, NM: Sunstone Press, 1987. 48p.

A boy grows up, secure and happy, in the house of his grandparents with two uncles, an aunt, and big sister, learning from his grandfather the things he needs to know to be a responsible adult in his Indian pueblo.

Walter, Mildred Pitts. **Trouble's Child.** West Caldwell, NJ: Lothrop, Lee & Shepard, 1985. 128p.

A coming-of-age story in which a young black woman must decide whether to adhere to her grandmother's wishes by remaining in the community and learning midwifery or to leave her island home and seek higher education.

Yep, Laurence. **Child of the Owl.** Scranton, PA: Harper & Row, 1977. 224p.

When Casey's irresponsible father is hospitalized, she is sent to her Chinese-speaking grandmother, who teaches Casey about her Chinese heritage and about love and responsibility.

Nonfiction Materials on Relatives and Extended Families

BOOKS

Bengston, Vern L., and Joan F. Robertson, editors. **Grandparenthood.** Beverly Hills, CA: Sage, 1985. 240p.

This book offers a broad perspective of the topic, including different ethnic groups and their customs, divorced families, styles and strategies of grandparents, and parent-adult-child relationships.

Cherlin, Andrew J., and Frank F. Furstenberg, Jr. **The New American Grandparent: A Place in the Family, a Life Apart.** New York: Basic Books, 1986. 278p.

After interviewing 510 grandparents and grandchildren, the authors wrote about different styles of grandparenting, the influence on grandchildren, changes through divorce in the family, potential financial problems, and the independent life versus dependency.

Dodson, Fitzhugh, with Paula Reuben. **How To Grandparent.** New York: Harper & Row, 1981. 290p.

Discusses special aspects of grandparenting, including gift giving and becoming desensitized to problem situations. The authors believe grandparents provide a unique kind of emotional involvement: that of part-time parents without pressure.

Galinsky, Ellen, and William H. Hooks. **The New Extended Family: Day Care That Works.** Photographs by Ellen Galinsky. Boston: Houghton Mifflin, 1977. 280p.

Young parents, trying to be independent, sometimes separate themselves from their families. Stepping outside the family has become an admission of failure. The authors argue that day care is part of the extended family and describe various care arrangements, from cooperatives to school-centered to home-centered.

Greenfield, Eloise, and Little, Lessis Jones. **Childtimes: A Three-Generational Memoir.** New York: Harper/Crowell, 1979. 175p.

As Greenfield reminisces, the lives of her mother and her grandmother are told in a loosely ordered, century-long collage of growing up black in America.

Kornhaber, Arthur. **Between Parents and Grandparents.** New York: St. Martin's Press, 1986. 158p.

The author examines the relationships between generations and the special place each has in the development of the child. Grandparents can be wizards, cronies, and heroes, with grandmothers playing a different role from grandfathers. Problems that arise from remarriage, stepgrandparenting, and jealous parents are discussed.

Kornhaber, Arthur, and Kenneth L. Woodward. **Grandparents/ Grandchildren: The Vital Connection.** Garden City, NY: Doubleday, 1981. 279p.

Through a questionnaire and interviews, the authors have drawn conclusions about what grandparents and grandchildren mean to one another, with an emotional history of today's grandparents and an agenda for them. The interview text and survey formats appear in the Appendix. Bibliography included.

LeShan, Eda. **Grandparents: A Special Kind of Love.** Riverside, NJ: Macmillan, 1984. 112p.

Using a warm, personable style, LeShan explores the unique relationship between grandchildren and grandparents, and offers advice to children on how they can best enjoy and appreciate their grandparents.

Richardson, Frank Howard. **Grandparents and Their Families: A Guide for Three Generations.** New York: David McKay, 1964. 116p.

Advice is given on how to establish fine, enjoyable relations among parents, grandparents, and children.

Streich, Corrine, editor. **Grandparents' Houses: Poems about Grandparents.** New York: Greenwillow, 1984. 30p.

This book presents 15 poems about grandfathers and grandmothers by poets from China, Japan, the United States, and other countries.

Townsend, Maryann, and Ronnie Stern. **Pop's Secret.** With black and white photographs. Reading, MA: Addison-Wesley, 1980. 26p.

A true story about a boy's love for his grandfather and deep grief after the old man dies. Mark responds favorably to his mother's suggestion that they make a book about Pop so none of the memories will be lost—a useful idea that could be extended to other areas of children's lives.

U.S. Senate. **The Extended Family: Society's Forgotten Resources.** Washington, DC: U.S. Government Printing Office, 1982.

A report on a hearing before the Senate subcommittee on Aging, Family and Human Services. The hearing was designed to gather information on the current status of the extended family, to recognize influences that prevent its full use as part of our country's helping network, and to examine measures that can be taken to enhance its role.

ARTICLE

Tice, Carol H. **"Perspectives on Intergenerational Initiatives: Past, Present and Future,"** *Children Today* 14, no. 5 (September/October 1985): 6, 7, 11, 26.

Children used to learn about what was expected of them at each stage of growth by being with people in different age groups. U.S. society today does not foster much merging of generations. Activities that encourage cross-generation interactions are discussed.

Nonprint Materials on Relatives and Extended Families

The Electric Grandmother

Type:	16mm film, 3/4" or 1/2" video
Length:	49 min.
Cost:	Rental $12
Distributor:	Learning Corporation of America
	108 Wilmot Road
	Deerfield, IL 60015
Date:	1982

A young father and his three children are visited by a near-human mechanical grandmother after the death of their wife and mother. Based on the story "I Sing the Body Electric" by Ray Bradbury; stars Maureen Stapleton and Edward Hermann.

Families: Teaching and Learning

Type:	Various video formats
Length:	15 min.
Cost:	Purchase, no amount indicated
Distributor:	Churchill Films
	622 N. Robertson Boulevard
	Los Angeles, CA 90069
Date:	1976

Children learn various skills from parents, grandparents, and each other. Support materials available.

Family Matters

Type:	16mm film or video
Length:	29 min.
Cost:	Rental $14, purchase $335 (film); rental $14, purchase $150 (video)
Distributor:	Cornell University
	A-V Resource Center, Media Services
	8 Research Park
	Ithaca, NY 14850
Date:	1984

Two families' situations are depicted: a single black mother accepts support from neighbors, while a white couple goes to live with her mother.

Home To Stay

Type:	1/2" VHS video
Length:	47 min.
Cost:	Rental $12
Distributor:	Time-Life Video
	Time & Life Building
	1271 Avenue of the Americas
	New York, NY 10020
Date:	1979

Henry Fonda stars as a spirited grandfather fighting off recurrent lapses into senility and the specter of a nursing home with the help of his fiercely loyal granddaughter Sarah. Adapted from Janet Majerus' novel, *Grandpa and Frank*. From the series The Teenage Years.

Mandy's Grandmother

Type:	16mm film, 3/4″ or 1/2″ video
Length:	30 min.
Cost:	Rental $12, purchase $545 (film); purchase $310 (video)
Distributor:	Phoenix/BFA Films and Video, Inc.
	470 Park Avenue South
	New York, NY 10016
Date:	1978

Based on the book by Liesel Moak Skorpen. Tomboy Mandy and her prim grandmother forget the disappointment of their first meeting and become friends. Maureen O'Sullivan portrays the grandmother.

The Secret Life of T. K. Dearing

Type:	16mm film, 2 reels
Length:	26 min., 20 min.
Cost:	Rental $12 each reel
Distributor:	Time-Life Video
	Time & Life Building
	1271 Avenue of the Americas
	New York, NY 10020
Date:	1980

A young girl, T. K. Dearing (played by Jodie Foster), develops a sensitive relationship with her grandfather. At first resentful when he comes to live with the family, T. K. learns that being old has almost as many problems and virtues as being young. From the series The Teenage Years.

Who Cares?

Type:	Various video formats
Length:	13 min.
Cost:	Purchase, no amount indicated
Distributor:	Sterling Educational Films
	241 E. 34th Street
	New York, NY 10016
Date:	1971

After creating conflict among members of his daughter's family with whom he has come to stay, a grumpy grandfather is led to ask where an aging person can look for comfort.

Organizations Concerned with Relatives and Extended Families

American Association of Retired Persons (AARP)
Special Projects: Intergenerational Activities
1909 K Street NW
Washington, DC 20049
(202) 872-4700
Director: Sandra Sweeney

The association provides program materials, including a film, to help children understand aging and is developing materials on grandparents' rights.

PUBLICATIONS: *Growing Together* (brochure), *Modern Maturity* (monthly).

Foster Grandparents Program
806 Connecticut Avenue NW, Room M-1006
Washington, DC 20525
(800) 424-8867
Acting Assistant Director: Marianne Klink

A program of ACTION, an independent government agency, that organizes older, low-income persons to act as foster grandparents who help provide person-to-person activities for the emotional, mental, and physical well-being of children with special or exceptional needs.

PUBLICATION: *Directory: Foster Grandparents Program.*

Intergenerational Clearinghouse
(Retired Senior Volunteer Program of Dane County, Inc.)
517 N. Segoe Road
Madison, WI 53705
(608) 238-7787
Director: Mary Stamstad

The clearinghouse works with over 30 schools in the area to provide grandparent tutors and "room" grandparents, and to help provide folk fairs and folklore and craft workshops in schools. Committees of parents, teachers, and older persons meet to plan activities. Provides information on intergenerational programs and activities throughout the country.

PUBLICATION: Newsletter (semiannual with national distribution).

CHAPTER 5

Families with One Child, Families with Siblings

> Trav was wearing a wine-colored blazer and dark pants, spit-shined shoes. . . . He was poised there on the bottom step, and I thought he'd just tell us to come on up to his room and get away from the perfect party. The concept of having your own room with your own door on it intrigued me somewhat.
>
> Richard Peck, *Remembering the Good Times*
> (New York: Dell, 1985), 41.

Trav, a single child, is a good student and seems to have all the material possessions he could want. But Trav is not happy and his friends and family are left to wonder why.

> My sister was so man-crazy it made me sick. And what if she got pregnant? Or left home? Or got married? I couldn't stand to think about it. The house would be a morgue without her. And, all my life she was my protector. As number 1 girl fighter of Shamrock, when she told the older guys to lay off me, they listened.
>
> Danny Santiago, *Famous All Over Town* (New York:
> New American Library, 1983), 42.

Fourteen-year-old Chato's curiosity about his older sister Lena and her activities includes reading her diary. The expectation in his culture is that he will protect her and be her chaperone, yet she protects him. Both Lena and Chato conspire to outwit their father, whom they feel is unduly harsh on them and their mother.

Statistics about Family Size

The size of families in the United States today represents a shift from previous times. For most of our nation's history, families with a single child were considered odd. Children were part of the economic vitality of the family, helping with chores and field work and working in factories to add to the family income. Even when relatively good birth control measures became available in the nineteenth century, most families preferred to have several children, especially since many children did not live to reach adulthood. Having more children helped ensure that some of them would mature, become productive economically, and support their parents and relatives when the older people could no longer work.

During the Baby Boom, from the late 1940s through the early 1960s, most families had at least two or three children. An only child was considered unusual, and even an object of pity. Today, however, the number of one-child families is increasing. In 1985 there were 13 million children without brothers or sisters. This represents a 50 percent increase over 1965 figures (Kantrowitz, 66). Average family size overall decreased 13.1 percent from 1960 to 1987 (U.S. Census figure).

Families with One Child

The terms *single child* and *only child* are used interchangeably in the literature about families; some sociologists feel *only child* has a negative connotation.

MYTHS ABOUT THE SINGLE CHILD

Because being a single child was considered strange in early times, a number of myths have grown up around children without siblings.

> Myth 1: Single children are spoiled and selfish. Studies show that single children do not differ from other children in sharing or cooperative behavior. In some instances they are more generous and trusting since they have not had to worry about competition (Hawke and Knox, 24).

> Myth 2: Single children are overly dependent. Single children are more often found to be self-confident and independent

rather than "shrinking violets." A study of college-age single children found them slightly better adjusted than other students, with no indications that they were more dependent on their parents (ibid., 26).

Myth 3: Single children are lonely. According to the studies, single children had as many close friends as other children, felt as popular, and spent about the same amount of time alone as children with siblings (ibid., 27).

Myth 4: Single children are underachievers. Some people maintain the lack of competition and stimulation from siblings creates a lack of motivation on the part of single children, but there is no evidence of a direct cause-effect link. In fact, the parents of the single child often value academic success and take time to encourage their child to do well. Language ability is one aspect of achievement where the single child is often superior, which may in turn influence achievement in other school subjects (ibid., 29).

Myth 5: Single children are maladjusted and unhappy. Single children and children with siblings show no apparent difference in qualities of happiness or adjustment. However, young people who had siblings believed that single children were more maladjusted. When single children were asked if they thought there were advantages in being a single child, every respondent under age 18 answered "yes" and 86 percent of the single-child adults agreed (ibid., 31).

SINGLE CHILDREN: THE REALITIES

Although it is difficult to generalize, research suggests that single children share some common characteristics.

1. Single children have more possessions and opportunities. Having a room of one's own is commonly mentioned as an asset by single children, but single-child adults remember more musical instruments and lessons, travel experiences, and educational opportunities than individuals with siblings. The respondents who described themselves as "spoiled" attributed the problem not to the possessions themselves, but to the motivation of parents who gave gifts to "buy their affection." However, this statement could also be true for parents of children who are siblings (ibid., 32).

2. Single children receive more parental attention. In the interviews with single children, this statement was regarded as a plus by some and a negative by others. How this attention is given is the key to whether it is advantageous or destructive (ibid., 33).

3. Single children miss the pleasures—and detriments—of siblings. Siblings can form wonderful relationships with each other, becoming best friends and companions, but this is not always true. When single children wonder what it would be like to have a sibling, many imagine a brother or sister who is warm and supportive, rather than considering the rivalry and jealousy which sometimes dominates sibling relationships (ibid., 35).

4. Single children are more adultlike. Single children are exposed more often to the adult social world and involved at an earlier age in adult activities. They may dine out, travel, and attend events like concerts and sports events more often, thus learning early in life how to behave and function in the adult world. Single children may develop a pseudo-sophistication and the appearance of wisdom beyond their years as a result of having a more mature vocabulary and behavior patterns. This can present a hazard for the child whose behavior is advanced beyond his/her chronological age. When such a child "acts his age," it can be a disappointment to the parents who have learned to expect more mature behavior (ibid., 37).

CHARACTERISTICS OF SINGLE CHILDREN

As infants, single children appear to acquire basic socialization more quickly, while in the middle years of childhood, they often show exceptional adjustment, independence, and good behavior. In adolescence, they are less likely to be absorbed by the superficial conformity of their peers or involved in disruptive rebellion. Teenage single children are more likely to retain the values of their parents than to become life-style rebels (Ellen Peck, 4).

Because the number of children in a household divide adult attention and involvement, the demands of more children may prevent the intimacy possible when there is a single child. The single child is welcomed into a special kind of household, nurtured in an atmosphere where love and attention and stimulation are often the expectation and where the child may be relatively free of insecurities. On the negative side, a recent *Newsweek* story relates a concern for the number of affluent two-career couples with a single child who expect perfection from the child (Kantrowitz, 67). The effect of this attitude on the child has not yet been adequately measured.

Ellen Peck relates that if a group of select or distinguished individuals is surveyed, there will be an overrepresentation of single children. In a group not entirely composed of distinguished individuals, the most outstanding members will still be single children (Ellen Peck, 22). A study of cover personalities of *Time* magazine during the years 1957 to 1968 found a larger percentage of men and women who are single children represented on the covers than would be expected in the general population (ibid.). Peck reports the same is true of contemporary arts critics, sports figures, Pulitzer Prize winning reporters, and general achievement as represented in *Who's Who*. Recognizing that it is not entirely a matter of "the best and brightest" couples who tend to have single children, Peck acknowledges the importance of education and other environmental factors.

ALONENESS

Thinking about their experiences as single children, many adults remember being alone a great deal. This can be both an advantage and a disadvantage since aloneness may help individuals become more creative. Silvano Arieti, author of *The Will To Be Human*, says that aloneness frees a person from constant exposure to the "conventions and cliches of life" so that an individual and unique vision may be developed and explored (Ellen Peck, 69). Peck stresses that one can be alone, but not feel alone. Solitude can be a "good habit" in terms of having time to read, think, and daydream. Imagination allows great things to take place, such as the creation of literature, and being alone provides time to remember and replay the past (ibid., 70).

Families with Siblings

Siblings have many opportunities to develop the life skills involved in getting along with people. They may even have "best friends" within their own families. Many families, although not without strife in the growing up years, become closer and more caring as the children mature.

FAMILY SIZE

There is no such thing as an ideal size for a family. Ideal for one family might be three children, for another five, for another just one. Some parents plan "cluster births," with the children close together in age to provide sibling playmates. Other parents space the births of their children to encourage each child to develop as an individual.

FORMS OF RIVALRY

Carole and Andrew Calladine say that sibling rivalry takes a variety of forms. In one form a particular child is the "Heir Apparent." This child always gets (or seems to get) the most parental attention, while the other siblings play a secondary role to this family favorite (Calladine and Calladine, 17). An example of this is in the novel *Jacob Have I Loved,* by Katherine Paterson. Sara Louise feels inferior to her twin sister, Caroline, who she imagines is prettier and talented musically. Because she believes her parents are more responsive to Caroline, Sara Louise basks in self-pity.

Another form of sibling rivalry is the child who tries to win the parents' attentions and affections by outdoing or outsmarting a sibling. There is a constant sibling contest to see who will get more love or the "best" rating each day (Calladine and Calladine, 17).

POSITION IN THE FAMILY

As the one who has been displaced by later children, the firstborn child may express ambivalence and hostility about siblings. Firstborn children are less likely to say they prefer playing with their siblings to playing with other children. They are seen by both first- and laterborn children as bossier and more dominant than laterborn children (Dunn, 70).

According to a study of siblings' power tactics, cited by Dunn, "firstborn children attack, use status more, and bribe. Laterborns tend to sulk, pout, plead, cry, and appeal to parents for help. The more polite techniques of explaining, taking turns, and asking are perceived by most children as the strategies only of firstborn girls. This tendency reflects the way in which the girls model themselves on their mother" (Dunn, 71). Dunn acknowledges this is a hypothesis with too little evidence to support it, but it illustrates the kind of research on position in the family that is being conducted and the results that are being published.

Firstborns often complain that too much responsibility is given to them too early. They also complain that parents have higher expectations of them to excel and achieve. Because of this, however, most firstborns feel the family role forces them to develop into responsible people. Perhaps this is why the research on firstborns in college shows they are leaders and possess a high motivation to achieve (Calladine and Calladine, 183). A side benefit for firstborns is there are no hand-me-downs and they receive privileges first.

Middle children may have the most inherent struggle to find their place in the family. They define their position mainly through comparisons with the other children: they have less responsibility than the oldest and are less spoiled than the youngest. It is harder for the middle child to feel special, and it is possible for them to drift in and out of the family.

Academic researchers find middles to be easy-going and good-natured joiners, but the Calladines say not many middles felt good about their family position (ibid., 185). Many said they would trade places with another sibling, feeling the first- or lastborn siblings receive better parental treatment. It may make a difference in how the middle child feels about family placement if he is the only boy, or she is the first girl.

The majority of lastborns feel good about their family position. From that secure position, they can observe and learn about growing up. There is no one following them to push them out of that placement. The family baby gets the most attention. Their parents feel more relaxed, while older siblings help to plan activities or play with them. They can become masters in getting their way (ibid., 184). Negative aspects of being lastborn include having too many bosses, dealing with parent and teacher expectations to be like older brothers and sisters, and being teased about being the baby. Nevertheless, lastborns usually feel special and well-loved.

PARENTS AND GENDER PREFERENCE

An open preference by a parent or parents as to the sex of a child can profoundly influence both the child's development and his or her relationship with siblings of the opposite sex. Such children may reflect these parental preferences by being uncertain about themselves and their roles. A lifelong search for recognition and identity can result from a parent wanting a boy child and having a girl, or vice versa. A daughter who perceives that her brothers are more important in her family, for example, may take out her feelings on her brothers, feel inferior to her brothers, or try to act like a boy. A boy could have similar problems if he feels his sister is favored by their parents. He might feel uncomfortable with people of his own sex, which could result in problems with the opposite sex as he grows up (McDermott, 82).

Society has tended to reinforce feelings of superiority in boys and inferiority in girls. Today, however, a shift is occurring. More and more, while the sexes are still considered quite different from each other, neither is better or more valued than the other. This transition period may be more difficult for boys to adjust to than girls.

LIVING WITH A HANDICAPPED SIBLING

Betsy Byars, author of *The Summer of the Swans,* describes the agony of 14-year-old Sara, who has to take care of her younger retarded brother. She doesn't want her friends to see her with him, but when he gets lost one night, Sara realizes how much she loves him.

Siblings may worry about having a brother or sister who is different in some way. The other children may be given certain responsibilities for the handicapped sibling, which can be a growth experience for the normal child. Handicapped children may not be competitive in the usual sense, but they may require more parental attention, taking time away from other children in the family. Studies on the stress level of siblings of handicapped children show that having open discussion of the handicap and allowing children to express their curiosity and feelings enables them to cope more effectively.

REFERENCES

Byars, Betsy. *The Summer of the Swans.* New York: Viking, 1970.

Calladine, Carole, and Andrew Calladine. *Raising Siblings.* New York: Delacorte, 1979.

Dunn, Judy. *Sisters and Brothers.* Cambridge, MA: Harvard University Press, 1985.

Hawke, Sharryl, and David Knox. *One Child by Choice.* Englewood Cliffs, NJ: Prentice-Hall, 1977.

Kantrowitz, Barbara. "Only But Not Lonely," *Newsweek* 107, no. 24 (16 June 1986): 66–67.

McDermott, John F., Jr. *Raising Cain (and Abel Too): The Parents' Book of Sibling Rivalry.* New York: Wyden Books, 1980.

Paterson, Katherine. *Jacob Have I Loved.* New York: Crowell, 1980.

Peck, Ellen. *The Joy of the Only Child*. New York: Delacorte, 1977.

Peck, Richard. *Remembering the Good Times*. New York: Dell, 1985.

Santiago, Danny. *Famous All Over Town*. New York: New American Library, 1983.

Statistical Abstract of the United States, 1988: National Data Book and Guide to Sources, 108th edition. Washington, DC: Government Printing Office, 1987.

Resources
for Finding Out about Only Children and Siblings

Fiction about Only Children and Siblings

Brooks, Bruce. **The Moves Make the Man.** New York: Harper & Row, 1984. 252p.

A sharp contrast is drawn between the family life of the narrator, Jeremy, a bright black boy in a fatherless but happy and adjusted home, and Bix, an excellent athlete who lives with his stepfather and whose mother is in a hospital for the mentally ill. Bix is an only child from an affluent home and feels a responsibility to be perfect and truthful in whatever he does.

Byars, Betsy. **The Summer of the Swans.** New York: Viking, 1970. 142p.

Fourteen-year-old Sara is given responsibility for her mentally retarded brother Charlie, and when he gets lost one night, she learns how much she loves him. Sibling relationships with a "different" sibling are handled sensitively.

Cormier, Robert. **The Bumblebee Flies Anyway.** New York: Pantheon, 1983, 241p.

Barney Snow lives in the Complex, an experimental hospital for terminally ill people. Mazzo, who is a patient in the hospital, and his twin sister Cassie are key players in Barney's efforts to make sense of the secret of the bumblebee and the reality of their situation.

Elfman, Blossom. **The Sister Act.** New York: Bantam, 1978. 151p.

Eighteen-year-old Molly, who is bright and talented, has to put her life on hold because of her beautiful but dumb younger sister who can't say no to the boys, hates school, and gets depressed. Momma wants to keep both of the girls home and is unrealistic about their maturity. Molly feels trapped, but finally makes decisions about her own life.

Girion, Barbara. **A Tangle of Roots.** Scribner's, 1976. 154p.

An only child, 16-year-old Beth feels responsible for her father after her mother dies suddenly of a cerebral hemorrhage. She neglects her friends to help him, but she learns to consider them and her own life.

Hinton, S. E. **The Outsiders.** New York: Viking, 1967. 188p.

With court permission, three brothers, ages 14, 17, and 20, live alone in the poor section of town after the death of their parents. They and their friends are involved in violent confrontation with a gang of wealthier boys. The book emphasizes the closeness and companionship among the youths, revealing that their tough exteriors hide other feelings.

————. **Tex.** New York: Delacorte, 1979. 194p.

Tex, 14, and his brother Mace, 16, live primarily by themselves, with only occasional visits from their rodeo-circuit rider father. Conflicts arise as they must accept responsibility for themselves while trying to remain typical high school students. As they struggle, their relationship grows through their love and need for each other.

Klein, Norma. **Confessions of an Only Child.** Illustrated by Richard Cuffari. New York: Pantheon, 1974. 93p.

Antonia, aged 9, and her best friend Libby think babies are a nuisance, based on Libby's experiences, but Antonia gradually adjusts to the idea of not being an only child. After Antonia's brother is born prematurely and dies, she learns to cope with her guilt and is ready to accept a sibling by the time the next baby is born. Although written for younger children, this is something of a landmark book on the topic.

Lowry, Lois. **A Summer To Die.** New York: Bantam, 1979. 154p.

Meg feels guilty about her sister Molly's illness and death because she argued with her and felt jealous of Molly's outgoing personality and popularity at school. However, life is affirmed for Meg through her friendship with a couple who are expecting a baby and her own interest and skill in photography.

MacLauchlan, Patricia. **Sarah, Plain and Tall.** New York: Harper & Row, 1985. 58p.

Caleb doesn't remember Mama, who died the day after he was born, but he and his older sister Anna are very interested in Sarah, who answers Papa's ad in the newspaper for a wife. The children agree to act especially nice and keep clean so Sarah will like them.

Paterson, Katherine. **Bridge to Terabithia.** Illustrated by Donna Diamond. New York: Crowell, 1977. 128p.

Giving insight into the lives of two young people, their imaginative world, and their families, the author acquaints the reader with Jess, the only boy in a family of girls, and Leslie, a girl and the only child in a family whose values and life-style are different from other families in the area. A sensitive and beautiful story of the friendship between Jess and Leslie as well as their family roles.

————. **Jacob Have I Loved.** New York: Crowell, 1980. 215p.

Living with her family on a small island in Chesapeake Bay, Sara Louise feels her twin sister Caroline is the pretty, talented, and popular child while she is filled with self-pity and jealousy. This is a Newbery Award book in which Sara Louise finally achieves her own identity and finds happiness with her own life choices. The title is a reminder of twins Jacob and Esau in the Bible, whom the nasty grandmother used to taunt Sara Louise about her jealousy.

Peck, Robert Newton. **A Day No Pigs Would Die.** New York: Dell, 1972, 139p.

Twelve-year-old Rob is the only child of a Shaker family on a farm in Vermont in the Depression. The story shows the pleasure of his simple life, along with his observations of school, nature, and life around him, and his ingenuity in coping with unusual circumstances on the farm. When his father dies, he has to become the man of the family.

Pevsner, Stella. **And You Give Me a Pain, Elaine.** Somers, CT: Seabury Press, 1978. 182p.

Elaine is the 16-year-old "mixed-up" sister in this story, which is narrated by 13-year-old Andrea. Elaine's weird friends, her frequent absences from home, and her constant arguments with her parents lead to her running away from home. Andrea feels left out because her parents don't have time to pay attention to her, and her older brother Joe is away at college. Elaine and her parents go for counseling to help solve their problems.

Richard, Adrienne. **Into the Road.** Boston: Atlantic Monthly Press, 1976. 206p. Available on cassette for the blind.

Nearing high school graduation, orphaned Nat is persuaded by his older brother to buy a motorcycle and travel with him for the summer. His encounter with a tough motorcycle gang and the motorcycling life broaden his outlook and clarify his values. He learns how he differs from his brother while gaining a new understanding and respect for him.

Santiago, Danny. **Famous All over Town.** New York: New American Library, 1983. 285p.

A Chicano family in an East Los Angeles barrio finds its neighborhood threatened with extinction by a railroad that wants the property. Written with humor and pathos, the story is told through the eyes of 14-year-old Chato and emphasizes family relationships, many of them related to the Chicano culture. The disintegration of the family, the neighborhood, and the culture are parallel themes.

Sharmat, Marjorie. **He Noticed I'm Alive . . . and Other Hopeful Signs.** New York: Delacorte, 1984. 146p.

Two years ago, Jody's mother left a note saying she was going to travel to "find herself," leaving 15-year-old Jody and her father to fend for themselves. As an only child, Jody has learned to be self-sufficient, cooking for and entertaining her friends.

Sleator, William. **Singularity.** New York: Bantam, 1985. 198p.

Harry feels dominated by his twin brother Barry, which creates strong feelings of jealousy between them. Alone in an old farm house, the boys discover a passageway to another universe and a time warp. Harry figures out how long he would have to be in the small house in order to become a year older than Barry and not have to put up with Barry's superior attitudes. A suspenseful fantasy that confronts sibling emotions in an interesting way.

Spinelli, Jerry. **Who Put That Hair in My Toothbrush?** Boston: Little, Brown, 1984. 220p.

The sibling rivalry between 12-year-old Megin and her older brother Greg intensifies after she ruins his science project and he retaliates by throwing her favorite hockey stick into the pond.

Voigt, Cynthia. **Dicey's Song.** New York: Fawcett, 1982. 211p.

The sequel to *Homecoming*. Both books reflect the warm, caring relationship a family of children have with each other after they are left to fend for themselves. They finally win over their grandmother as well.

Winthrop, Elizabeth. **A Little Demonstration of Affection.** New York: Harper & Row, 1975. 152p.

Coming from a family that does not display affection, 13-year-old Jenny overreacts to her 14-year-old brother's hug. Her guilty feelings confuse her until a talk with her father explains the naturalness and normality of her feelings. This is a powerful and unsettling novel about a family's deepest feelings.

Nonfiction Materials on Only Children and Siblings

BOOKS

Ames, Louise Bates, with Carol Chase Haber and the Gesell Institute of Human Development. **He Hit Me First: When Brothers and Sisters Fight.** New York: Dembner, 1982. 190p.

Focusing on fighting between siblings, this book includes a discussion of how each child's position in the family influences behavior. Chapter 12 discusses changes in behavior that come about with age and the outlook for future relationships between siblings.

Arnstein, Helene S. **Brothers and Sisters/Sisters and Brothers.** New York: Dutton, 1979. 239p.

In a comprehensive book on siblings, the author deals with the impact brothers and sisters have on each other's lives and explains the power struggles, rivalries, guilts, fears, and dependencies as well as the sharing, self-confidence, and love rooted in early childhood patterns. The author refers to famous siblings such as the Marx brothers, the Kennedy clan and the children of Joan Crawford.

Calladine, Carole, and Andrew Calladine. **Raising Siblings: A Sane and Sensible Approach to Raising Brothers and Sisters without Raising the Roof.** New York: Delacorte, 1979. 208p.

The authors are professional counselors and group therapists who advocate parents treat each child as an only child, responding to individual needs and not worrying about being "fair." They promote the idea of a family judicial system and provide specific steps for family activities and discipline.

Dunn, Judy. **Sisters and Brothers: The Developing Child Series.** Cambridge, MA: Harvard University Press, 1985. 182p.

Dunn argues that in fighting, bullying, or comforting, siblings possess a deeper understanding of others than psychologists have supposed. She challenges the usual assumptions that birth order, age gap, and gender are the most crucial factors in explaining differences between siblings within a family and suggests that siblings themselves have an important influence on each other's development.

Faber, Adele, and Elaine Mazlish. **Siblings without Rivalry: How To Help Your Children Live Together So You Can Live Too.** Illustrations by Kimberly Ann Coe. New York: W. W. Norton, 1987. 219p.

Based on experiences of real parents, the authors have developed ways to reduce the antagonism between siblings. Vivid dialog and cartoons illustrate the many forms of sibling rivalry and show how to promote cooperation rather than competition, how to be fair and not just equal, and how to be helpful to both the "bully" and the "victim."

Hawke, Sharryl, and David Knox. **One Child by Choice.** Englewood Cliffs, NJ: Prentice-Hall, 1977. 233p.

Suggesting the single-child family is an option every couple should consider, the authors show why life-style, inflation, and worldwide overpopulation make this a reasonable decision. Based on both original research and previous studies, the book explores the myths and realities concerning single-child families.

McDermott, John F., Jr. **Raising Cain (and Abel Too): The Parents' Book of Sibling Rivalry.** New York: Wyden Books, 1980. 240p.

In this guide a child psychiatrist tells parents how to influence competition and fighting between siblings, activities he feels help children to develop a special identity, and a sense of who and what they are and their place in the family network. Using scenarios, the author illustrates how parents tend to handle situations, followed by how they should handle them.

Peck, Ellen. **The Joy of the Only Child.** New York: Delacorte, 1977. 243p.

After reviewing recent research, Peck concludes that the only child tends to come out on the plus side in physical health and strength, intelligence, social and moral responsibility, creativity, character traits, and sexual adjustment. She also found parents with one child felt less financial strain, were more relaxed, had better senses of humor, and had more time for their own development.

Rofes, Eric E., and the students at Fayerweather Street School. **The Kids' Book about Parents.** Boston: Houghton Mifflin, 1984. 204p.

Written by the children at the Fayerweather Street School in Cambridge, Massachusetts, who give their perspective on various kinds of families. One section deals with the "Problems and Rewards of Living in Different Kinds of Families," such as nuclear, extended, guardian, stepfamily, and commune. Those who are the only child in the family wrote about the advantages and disadvantages of their situations, while other children wrote about getting along with siblings.

Shyer, Marlene Fanta. **Here I Am, an Only Child.** Pictures by Donald Carrick. New York: Scribner's, 1985. Unpaged.

Delightful picture book that recounts the good and bad parts of being an only child. It has universal appeal.

Strean, Herbert S., and Lucy Freeman. **Raising Cain: How To Help Your Children Achieve a Happy Sibling Relationship.** New York: Facts on File Publications, 1988. 175p.

Strean, a child therapist, and Freeman believe that siblings mirror the parents' relationship with each other as well as the parents' own sibling relationships. The effects of birth order, age difference, and family size on the siblings are discussed, as are special relationships between adopted siblings, stepsiblings, and twins.

ARTICLE

Kantrowitz, Barbara. **"Only but Not Lonely,"** Newsweek 107, no. 24 (16 June 1986): 66–67.

The author discusses changing views of the one-child household, describes an increase of such families, and concludes that "onlies" may be brighter and more achievement-oriented than children in larger families.

Nonprint Materials on Only Children and Siblings

Boys and Girls
Type: ½" VHS video
Length: 25 min.

Cost:	Rental $12
Distributor:	Atlantis Productions Inc.
	1252 La Granada Drive
	Thousand Oaks, CA 91360
Date:	1983

As her younger brother grows up, Margaret is frustrated with her parents' expectations of her and is denied the chance to work alongside her father. She identifies with the courage and individuality of a spirited mare. From the series Coming of Age.

Cages

Type:	1/2″ VHS video
Length:	26 min.
Cost:	Rental $12
Distributor:	Atlantis Productions Inc.
	1252 La Granada Drive
	Thousand Oaks, CA 91360
Date:	1985

A miner and his two sons, Gene and Billy, struggle to deal with the "cages" they have built for themselves. This family in conflict includes a rebellious, aimless teenager and his sensitive brother, who assumes a sort of guardianship, often at cost to himself. From the series Coming of Age.

Family Problems

Type:	Various video formats
Length:	12 min.
Cost:	Purchase, no amount indicated
Distributor:	Sterling Educational Films
	241 E. 34th Street
	New York, NY 10016
Date:	1971

A sister struggles with her loyalty while her family is thrown into a turmoil as she keeps her brother's secret.

Hey, What about Me?

Type:	Video
Length:	22 min.
Cost:	Purchase $79.95
Distributor:	Tucker/Murphy Associates
	Kidvidz
	618 Centre
	Newton, MA 02158
Date:	1987

Three about-to-be siblings voice their initial ambivalence over the
expected babies in their families.

Jamie: The Story of a Sibling

Type: Various video formats
Length: 28 min.
Cost: Purchase or rental, no amount indicated
Distributor: National Film Board of Canada
1251 Avenue of the Americas, 16th Floor
New York, NY 10020
Date: 1965

The pressures of sibling rivalry are critical during child development.
This program gives parents an insight into the tension involved and
focuses on the conflicts that may arise.

Oh Brother, My Brother

Type: Various video formats
Length: 14 min.
Cost: Purchase or rental, no amount indicated
Distributor: Pyramid Film and Video
Box 1048
Santa Monica, CA 90406
Date: 1980

The program focuses on two young brothers' love for each other,
capturing the conflict and joy they find in each other's presence. The
program won a gold medal from the Houston International Film
Festival and a *Learning* Magazine Learning Award.

Organization Concerned with Siblings

Organizations concerned with the family in general are included as
part of Chapter 1. The organization listed here has a concern for the
siblings of disabled individuals.

Sibling Information Network (Disabled)

Connecticut University's Affiliated Program on Developmental
Disabilities
991 Main Street East
Hartford, CT 06108
(203) 282-7050
Assistant Coordinator: Lisa Pappanikou

The membership includes families and professionals from many areas, all having an interest in the welfare of siblings of children with handicaps and issues related to families of individuals with handicaps. The network acts as a clearinghouse for research coordination and services regarding the siblings of persons with handicaps.

PUBLICATION: *Sibling Information Network Newsletter* (quarterly).

CHAPTER 6

Adoption

"My name is Natalie Armstrong. I am the child to whom you gave birth in September 1960 in Simmons' Mills. I am now seventeen years old. For the past two months I have been trying to find you. Now finally here I am a few blocks away from you, and I am at a loss about what I should do next. I don't want to disrupt your own life in any way.... But I want so much to see you, and to talk. Perhaps all these years you have been wondering, too, as I have."

Lois Lowry, *Find a Stranger, Say Goodbye* (Boston: Houghton Mifflin, 1978), 129–130.

Although Natalie knows she was adopted, she grows up in a happy home, and doesn't think much about her background until she is filling out college applications. Because of her curiosity about her birth parents, her adoptive parents give her money, a car, and time to search for her parents. The quote is from the letter she writes to her birth mother the day before they meet. Their meeting, full of tentative questions and reflecting anxiety on both sides, is perhaps more satisfying to both mother and daughter than is sometimes the case for the adopted child and birth parent.

"Do you know what I found out? It has fingernails now and can even suck its thumb if it wants to." Zee paused. "The book said it can even tell how its mother feels about it. You know, if she loves it or not.... Do you think it already knows I probably can't keep it, Hughie?"

Patricia Calvert, *Stranger, You and I* (New York: Scribner's, 1987), 100.

Zee's life has been in a turmoil since she found out she is pregnant. A junior in high school, she knows that she cannot keep the baby and provide a good life for it. The baby's father is a high school senior heading for college, with no thoughts of marriage. So Zee has made plans for the baby to be adopted, but the decision is a painful one.

Statistics about Adoption

Statistics on adoptions reflect current trends in adoption procedures:

- Adoptions in the United States by unrelated persons decreased from 54 percent in 1960 to 35 percent in 1982 (*Statistical Abstract, 1988,* 356).
- Adoptions by a relative, including stepfamilies and blood relatives, such as grandparents, uncles and aunts, increased from 46 percent in 1960 to 64 percent in 1982. These figures reflect a nationwide trend toward "blended families," where children from a previous marriage are adopted into their current home structure (ibid.).
- Foreign adoptions grew from 5,633 children in 1975 to 9,286 in 1985. Asian children represented 75 percent of these numbers, with 60 percent being infants (ibid.).
- The number of transracial black/white adoptions has increased significantly over the years, accounting for 20 to 35 percent of the nonrelative adoptive placements from 1969 to 1976 (Feigelman and Silverman, 12).

Adoption Practices Reflect Changing Family Life

William Feigelman and Arnold R. Silverman suggest that changes reflected in adoption practices are outgrowths of changing family life. These changes include:

Diminishing fertility and family size. Only two percent of married women said they prefer to be childless, but one of every six couples of childbearing age has an infertility problem (Lord et al., 59). Among couples who get medical help, two out of five still cannot produce their own babies, and for every healthy white infant who is up for adoption, there are 100 couples or singles seeking such a baby (ibid.).

The drop in fertility rates has increased the demand for adoptions and decreased the number of available children. Treatment for infertility is costly (estimated at $3,000 a couple), and the "gray" market, where babies are sold for large amounts of money, has been on the rise. The lack of availability of infants has encouraged the number of foreign adoptions and adoptions of hard-to-place children: those who are older, minority children, or those in less than good health.

The changing pattern of illegitimate births. There has not been a decline in the number of these births, but rather an increase in mothers' unwillingness to relinquish their infants for adoption. This is especially true for white teenage mothers, 65 percent of whom gave their babies for adoption in 1966 compared with only 18 percent in 1971. The social and sexual mores of society have changed, allowing single mothers to keep their infants without the social stigma that was once attached to such babies. The growing acceptance of single-parent families and economic benefits from parents or social services have also contributed to this trend. Black teenagers, however, have reversed this trend, with more black girls considering legal abortion or adoption for their illegitimate babies (Feigelman and Silverman, 17).

The postponement of marriage. The proportion of women waiting to marry and start families has had an apparent negative effect on fertility. More and more women are waiting till age 35 or later to try to become pregnant, and a fourth of them are failing—that is, they have tried for a year or more to achieve a successful pregnancy and haven't (Lord et al., 58). Using modern birth control methods may keep a couple from knowing of their infertility until it is too late to begin the lengthy procedures to reverse the condition. In the 1950s, an estimated one couple in ten had infertility problems; today it is one couple in six. Adoption is an alternative for such infertile couples.

The rising rate of divorce. The increase in divorces has helped make single-parent families more common and more accepted, which in turn has encouraged young unwed mothers to keep their babies. It has also led child welfare agencies to think more positively about single adults as potential adoptive parents. Placement of a child with a single parent is now considered vastly superior to having the child live in an institution or with a succession of foster parents.

Adoption as a moral choice. Some families, concerned about global overpopulation, choose to adopt an existing child, perhaps from an underdeveloped country, rather than add more children to the world.

These changes have encouraged agencies to reexamine some of their policies, including taking a closer look at serving the needs of children as opposed to being concerned about "matching" the potential parents and the child, as was standard operating procedure in the past. Advocates of children's rights claim children are entitled to permanent homes. There is also a question as to the point when a parent placing a child in foster care relinquishes parental rights.

The Adoptive Parents

In early times, acquisition of an heir was the only justification for adoption. Couples in some societies adopted a son or daughter to perform the sex-typed services of hunting or housekeeping, particularly in anticipation of the parents' old age. Today, however, people adopt for a variety of reasons. Most often the adopters are past the stage of reproduction or are infertile. In fact, proof of infertility used to be required as a qualification for adoption.

Although a majority of adoption cases today involve infertility, an increasing number of fertile parents are seeking to adopt children. Biological children of adoptive parents are more than twice as likely to have been born before the adoption as after. The parents may choose to adopt rather than have more children of their own because they do not wish to add to the global population, and/or in order to give their biological children the experience of sharing possessions and a close sibling relationship with another child.

In the past, couples who adopted were likely to be in their late twenties and early thirties, but recent surveys show a growing number of older couples are adopting children. Acceptance of adoption is greater among the more highly educated and affluent families and those bearing fewer children. Usually the adoptive parents are more successful economically than their nonadopting counterparts (Feigelman and Silverman, 13). Also more single adults, usually women, are becoming adoptive parents, and there are some instances of homosexual couples adopting children.

A substantial proportion of adoptions in America involve relatives. Circumstances such as accidents, death, career crises, emotional problems, or financial difficulties may necessitate that children grow up away from their biological families. In such cases relatives will often take the children rather than having them go to foster homes or be adopted by strangers. Adoptions by stepparents represent another significant percent of the total.

Families who want to adopt children who are not relatives may choose to work with an agency or to attempt an independent adoption. Agencies may be public or private; many are either church-related or government-funded. Agencies generally have extensive screening processes for parents and children and can provide references and credentials as well as handling the legalities. They usually charge the adoptive parents a fee for their services.

Because most agencies have long waiting lists, especially for white babies, many people are choosing to arrange independent adoptions. Prospective parents may advertise to find a pregnant teenager or other woman willing to give up her baby, offering to pay all of her birth-related expenses. Sometimes they make arrangements that include allowing the birth mother to have contact with the child. Independent adoptions are more flexible than agency-sponsored adoptions, but they can also be more risky for both the birth mother and the adoptive parents.

The Adoptee

Adopted children come in all ages, nationalities, and temperaments. Although data are incomplete, there is some evidence that points to a dramatic increase in the number of older and handicapped children who are being adopted.

The situation surrounding an adoption affects the ease or difficulty the child has in adjusting to a new home. Since many children are adopted as babies, the new home may be the first the child experiences after birth. The parents adapt to the baby's schedule and establish a routine, which makes it seem that the baby has always been theirs. It may be difficult for parents in this situation to acknowledge later to the child that he or she was adopted.

Evidence indicates children should be told of their adoption between the ages of three and five. If they are not told by age ten, they are likely to learn about it through playmates or in less desirable circumstances. Adoptees often feel shock and disbelief if they are not told before becoming an adolescent, which may result in anger toward their adoptive parents and/or birth parents. Discovering the fact of one's adoption through applying for a marriage license, finding a birth certificate, or at the death of an adoptive parent can be an unwelcome shock. Adoptees who have a satisfactory home life, however, tend to be the least disrupted by the revelation of their adoptive status.

Some adoptees seem more satisfied if they know about the birth parents and the circumstances of their adoption. Others are not concerned, feeling their lives are complete without this knowledge. Many adoptees express a keen interest in the circumstances of their adoption. They want to know the personal, social, and physical characteristics of their birth parents and why they gave them up. Adoptees see this information as important for themselves and for their own children.

There are procedures available now to help an adopted child find his or her birth parents. Legislatures, courts, and agencies have changed procedures and practices in an effort to accommodate the interests of adoptees, natural parents, and adoptive parents.

The identity of the biological parents was protected by law for many years, but social pressure from adoptees who felt they deserved to know more about their backgrounds helped change the legislation in many states. Adoptees are insisting on their rights to full disclosure of information about themselves and their genealogical origins. Part of this movement comes from expanded ethnic pride and need for self-knowledge, including health-related information.

For his book *In Search of Origins,* John Triseliotis interviewed 70 adults who came to the Register House in Edinburgh for information from their original birth records. A change in Scottish law made the interviews possible. Published in 1973, his landmark research is still widely cited. The group that volunteered for the study expressed a variety of reasons for their interest in learning more about their backgrounds.

Triseliotis arrived at three main conclusions that have implications for adoption practices:

1. The developing child has a need for a warm, caring and secure family life.
2. Adoptees are especially vulnerable to the experiences of loss, rejection, or abandonment.
3. Adopted persons need to know as much as possible about the circumstances of their adoption and about their genealogical background to integrate these facts into their developing personality (Triseliotis, 160).

The Biological Parents

Parents who give up their children for adoption can be of any age, socioeconomic level, and marital status. Children born out of wedlock constitute 87 percent of the nonrelative adoptions, according to a 1971 report by the National Center for Social Statistics (Feigelman and Silverman, 10).

Fears of the biological mother changing her mind about relinquishing her child haunt many adoptive parents. When the emotional attachment of the adoptive parents and adopted child is firm, the birth parents' role is subordinated. Although it is natural for the birth parent to be curious about the welfare of her child, it is not fair to disrupt the relationships that have been established in the adoptive home without some preparations.

The same kind of preparation needs to be made if adopted children want to have contact with their birth parents. If the child was born out of wedlock, the birth mother may have gotten married and had other children without divulging this secret about her past. If somebody appears and claims to be the child of the mother, it could be disastrous for the birth mother's entire family and for the adopted person as well.

In her book *To Love and Let Go,* Suzanne Arms details case studies of several young girls who were pregnant and decided to give their children to adoptive parents. Arms believes there should be more openness between the pregnant girl and the adoptive parents, saying "the key lies in giving people the information and support they need to face their limits honestly, and in offering kinds of adoptions that allow dignity" (Arms, 222).

A phenomenon that has become very controversial is surrogate motherhood, in which a woman is paid to bear a child for a couple who are unable to have children themselves. The child may be conceived with the sperm of the adoptive father, or through test-tube conception. In a few well-publicized cases, birth mothers decided not to give the child to the adoptive parents and court cases resulted, with a great deal of pain for all involved.

In her book *Surrogate Sister,* Eve Bunting tells the story of a widowed mother of a teenage girl who "helps out" a childless couple by having their baby for them. The mother felt she was doing something noble and good, but her daughter is embarrassed by the entire situation. The ethical questions involved in such cases have yet to be resolved. Some people are pushing for legislation to outlaw surrogate motherhood altogether, while others believe it is a private issue for people to resolve themselves.

Foster Home Care

Foster parents are people who provide temporary care in their homes for children who for various reasons cannot be cared for by their own parents. The decision to remove a child may be voluntary, as when a mother decides she does not have the resources to care for her children, or involuntary, as in cases of suspected child abuse. Children who are in foster homes are considered wards of the state, and the state pays the foster parents a stipend for the children's care.

States have laws that regulate the licensing of such facilities and require careful screening of foster parents and homes. A training program is usually involved to help the foster parents be as effective as possible. Each child is also assigned to a social worker who is responsible for supervising his or her care.

A child may be in a foster home anywhere from a few hours to several years. Some children are eventually adopted by their foster parents. Some critics of the foster care system believe the goal should be the eventual reuniting of biological parent and child; others believe foster care should be planned to develop a sense of permanence and stability in the child's life. Despite attempts to provide such stability, some children spend their lives moving through a succession of foster homes until they are old enough to be on their own. Gilly Hopkins in Katherine Paterson's novel, *The Great Gilly Hopkins*, has been in one foster home after another all her life. She has learned survival skills, but not all of them are socially acceptable. It is harder for such a child to make a transition to a successful, productive adult life.

REFERENCES

Arms, Suzanne. *To Love and Let Go*. New York: Knopf, 1983.

Bunting, Eve. *Surrogate Sister*. Philadelphia: Lippincott Jr. Books, 1984.

Calvert, Patricia. *Stranger, You and I*. New York: Scribner's, 1987.

Feigelman, William, and Arnold R. Silverman. *Chosen Children: New Patterns of Adoptive Relationships*. New York: Praeger, 1983.

Lord, Lewis J., et al. "Desperately Seeking Baby," *U.S. News & World Report* 103, no. 14 (5 October 1987): 58–64.

Lowry, Lois. *Find a Stranger, Say Goodbye*. Boston: Houghton Mifflin, 1978.

Paterson, Katherine. *The Great Gilly Hopkins*. New York: Avon, 1979.

Statistical Abstract of the United States, 1988: National Data Book and Guide to Sources, 108th edition. Washington, DC: Government Printing Office, 1987.

Triseliotis, John. *In Search of Origins: The Experiences of Adopted People*. Boston: Routledge & Kegan Paul, 1973.

Resources
for Finding Out about Adoption

Fiction about Adoption

Adler, Carole Schwerdtfeger. **The Cat That Was Left Behind.** Boston: Houghton Mifflin, 1981. 146p.

Thirteen-year-old Chad, spending a summer at Cape Cod with a new foster family, finds his life bearable because of the friendship of a cat. When his mother, who has been ill, writes and says she and her new husband don't want him to live with them, he is devastated. The foster family plans to adopt him.

Bates, Betty. **Bugs in Your Ears.** New York: Holiday House, 1977. 128p.

Thirteen-year-old Carrie has been adopted by her stepfather but yearns to know more about her "real" father who deserted the family when Carrie was a baby. Carrie struggles to get along with her new stepfamily and feels nobody listens to her because they have "bugs in their ears."

Bates, Betty. **It Must've Been the Fish Sticks.** New York: Holiday House, 1982. 136p.

Brian, an eighth grader and the son of a college president, is shocked when he finds out his real mother is alive. Nat, the black hired help, drives Brian to Ohio to meet his biological mother, Imogene, whose life-style is a marked contrast to Brian's. Her live-in boy friend races cars and lives off welfare.

Calvert, Patricia. **Stranger, You and I.** New York: Scribner's, 1987. 152p.

Zee, a junior in high school, learns she is pregnant after a one-night encounter with a senior boy she admires. Zee, who knows she must give the baby up for adoption, doesn't want to confront Jordie with his fatherhood, and appreciates Hugh's friendship and longing to help her. A warm and upbeat story told from Hugh's point of view.

Derby, Pat. **Visiting Miss Pierce.** New York: Farrar, Straus & Giroux, 1986. 133p.

Barry Wilson, a high school freshman, befriends 83-year-old Miss Pierce as part of his social concerns class. Living in the past, she thinks Barry is her dead brother. Through this relationship, Barry gets a new perspective on his own adoption.

First, Julia. **I, Rebekah, Take You, the Lawrences.** New York: Franklin Watts, 1981. 123p.

Having moved from orphanages to foster homes, 12-year-old Rebekah is cynical and reluctant to reveal her true emotions to the loving couple who want to adopt her. A compelling and satisfying story.

Lifton, Betty Jean. **I'm Still Me.** New York: Knopf, 1981. 243p.

When asked to write her family tree for a school assignment, 16-year-old Lori doesn't know how to get information on her birth parents and doesn't feel it is right to use her adoptive parents' background. This first-person narrative shows the turmoil some adoptive children feel about their identity.

Lowry, Lois. **Find a Stranger, Say Goodbye.** Boston: Houghton Mifflin, 1978. 187p.

Natalie isn't really curious about her biological mother until she is filling out college applications. Her foster parents provide her with a car, a bank account, and long weekends during the summer to search for her mother. After a lesson on parting with "psychological luggage," Natalie is happy with her decisions.

Miner, Jane Claypool. **Miracle of Time: Adopting a Sister.** Color illustrations by Vista III Design. Mankato, MN: Crestwood House, 1982. 63p.

A teenage girl reaches her emotionally scarred adoptive sister Kim, a five-year-old orphan from Vietnam. From the Crisis Series.

Myers, Walter Dean. **Won't Know Till I Get There.** New York: Viking, 1982. 176p.

Written in diary form by 14-year-old Steve and set in Harlem, the story is about Steve and his foster brother, Earl, who are assigned to work in a senior citizens' house as community service after committing vandalism. The reader gains insight into the boys' lives and the problems, concerns, and feelings of the old people.

Paterson, Katherine. **The Great Gilly Hopkins.** New York: Avon, 1979. 156p.

By the time she is 11 and in sixth grade, Gilly has been moved from one foster home to another, learning survival skills if nothing else. Finally she is placed with Mrs. Trotter, who though not too bright is full of love and teaches Gilly to care about others.

Pfeffer, Susan Beth. **About David.** New York: Delacorte, 1980. 167p.

David has killed his adoptive parents and committed suicide before the book starts. Seventeen-year-old Lynn tries to piece the parts together to determine why it happened, relating the story in diary form and providing the reader with insights.

————. **Just between Us.** New York: Delacorte, 1980. 116p.

Three young girls learn how important it is to keep secrets, including divorce and adoption information. A funny, warm, first-person narrative that will provide good discussion material.

Shyer, Marlene Fanta. **My Brother, the Thief.** New York: Scribner's, 1980. 138p.

Richard, 15, was adopted by Dr. Desmond, his stepfather, who sets high goals for all his children. Finally discovering how he is contributing to Richard's poor self-image, the doctor tries to be gentler with the children. The story is narrated by the doctor's 12-year-old daughter Carolyn, who tries to help her stepbrother.

Storr, Catherine Cole. **Vicky.** Winchester, MA: Faber and Faber, 1981. 152p.

An adopted teenager successfully traces her birth parents, but finds the knowledge by itself doesn't change her life. She is more appreciative of her adoptive family. A British flavor adds to the account.

Swartley, David Warren. **My Friend, My Brother.** Black and white illustrations by James Converse. Scottdale, PA: Herald Press, 1980. 102p.

With an emphasis on family communication and togetherness, this book describes the friendship between a Mennonite boy and his hardened, abused detractor who is adopted by an abusive uncle and aunt. Appropriate for easy reading for older children.

Nonfiction Materials on Adoption

BOOKS

Allen, Walter R. **Black American Families, 1965–1984: A Classified, Selectively Annotated Bibliography.** New York: Greenwood, 1986. 480p.

A comprehensive bibliography of information on the black American family, including a section on adoption. The key word index adds to the usefulness of the book.

Arms, Suzanne. **To Love and Let Go.** New York: Knopf, 1983. 228p.

The author relates in narrative form the stories of girls/women and their struggle to let go of someone they love. These are stories of mothers giving up children for various and personal reasons, out of love and respect for the child's needs. Concern for adoptive parents is an important factor in the stories.

Berman, Claire. **We Take This Child.** New York: Doubleday, 1974. 203p.

Based on interviews with specific families, this book examines the adoption of the handicapped child, the older child, and transracial and intercountry adoptions.

Bolles, Edmund Blair. **The Penguin Adoption Handbook.** New York: Viking, 1984. 253p.

The author offers strategies for those who wish to adopt but do not want to go through the "labyrinth" of agencies. Includes a directory of parent associations in each state.

Bunin, Catherine, and Sherry Bunin. **Is That Your Sister?** New York: Pantheon, 1976. 35p.

An adopted six-year-old girl tells about adoption and how she and her adopted sister feel about it.

Canape, Charlene. **Adoption: Parenthood without Pregnancy.** New York: Henry Holt, 1986. 246p.

The content describes the adoption process, including information on agency and independent adoption, adoptions by single parents, and adopting foreign or special-needs children. The appendix lists adoption agencies and support groups for parents.

Curto, Josephine J. **How To Become a Single Parent: A Guide for Single People Considering Adoption or Natural Parenthood Alone.** Englewood Cliffs, NJ: Prentice-Hall, 1983. 238p.

The process, problems, and special concerns for prospective single parents.

DuPrau, Jeanne. **Adoption: The Facts, Feelings and Issues of a Double Heritage.** New York: Messner, 1981. 127p.

Discusses the legal and emotional aspects of the adoption process and examines the current movement for giving adoptees free access to the records concerning their origins.

Dusky, Lorraine. **Birthmark.** New York: M. Evans, 1979. 191p.

The story of a birth mother's search for her child who had been placed for adoption.

Feigelman, William, and Arnold R. Silverman. **Chosen Children: New Patterns of Adoptive Relationships.** New York: Praeger, 1983. 261p.

Based on research conducted from 1973 to 1976, the authors discuss the changing patterns of adoption, including the causes, issues, and questions associated with them. Includes discussions on adopting hard-to-place or transracial children and single-parent adoptions.

Festinger, Trudy. **Necessary Risk: A Study of Adoptions and Disrupted Adoption Placements.** Washington, DC: Child Welfare League of America, 1986. 48p.

Children who are considered high risk in adoptions were the focus of this study aimed at determining what factors contributed to success or disruption of adoption placements. The author considers the outcomes for 482 children placed alone and 415 children placed in sibling groups in New York City.

Fisher, Florence. **The Search for Anna Fisher.** New York: A. Fields, 1973. 270p.

The biography of an adopted child and the frustrations she faced in trying to find her roots.

Gay, Kathlyn. **The Rainbow Effect: Interracial Families.** New York: Franklin Watts, 1987. 141p.

Uses interviews with members of interracial/interethnic families to explore problems faced by "mixed" children in such areas as family, school, dating, and adoption.

Gilman, Lois. **The Adoption Resource Book.** New York: Harper & Row, revised edition, 1987. 356p.

Gilman provides valuable information for potential adoptive parents, including advice and specific details on such topics as intercountry adoption and independent adoption.

Hormann, Elizabeth. **After the Adoption.** Old Tappan, NJ: F. H. Revell Co., 1987. 176p.

This book discusses the development of family relationships after an adoption has taken place.

Jewett, Claudia. **Adopting the Older Child.** Harvard, MA: Harvard Common Press, 1978. 308p.

This book tells the story of the Jewett family, who have seven adopted children and three biological children.

Johnston, Patricia Irwin. **An Adoptor's Advocate.** Fort Wayne, IN: Perspectives Press, 1984. 84p.

Psychological aspects of adoptions, childlessness in the United States, and the role of foster care and social workers.

Koh, Frances M. **Oriental Children in American Homes.** Minneapolis, MN: East-West Press, 1981. 132p.

Explores the special concerns involved in the adoptions of Oriental children by American families and the outcomes of such adoptions.

Kornheiser, Tony. **The Baby Chase.** New York: Atheneum, 1983. 212p.

Using his reporter's eye as he and his wife attempt an independent adoption, Kornheiser's wit and frustrations provide helpful background information for prospective parents.

Krementz, Jill. **How It Feels To Be Adopted.** New York: Knopf, 1982. 105p.

Using interviews with adopted children and adoptive families about their experiences and feelings concerning adoption, Krementz wrote this book especially for readers from seventh grade through adulthood.

Ladner, Joyce A. **Mixed Families: Adopting across Racial Boundaries.** Garden City, NY: Anchor Press/Doubleday, 1977. 290p.

Interviews with white parents and black children document a discussion of interracial adoption in the United States.

Lifton, Betty Jean. **Lost and Found: The Adoption Experience.** New York: Dial, 1979. 303p.

Offers insights into the experience of adoptees.

————. **Twice Born: Memoirs of an Adopted Daughter.** New York: McGraw-Hill, 1975. 281p.

A biography that focuses on adoption in the United States.

Macmanus, Sheila. **The Adoption Book.** New York: Hawthorn, 1975. 233p.

Baby selling, independent adoption, and sealed records are part of the variety of adoption issues included in this book.

McRoy, Ruth G., and Louis A. Zurcher, Jr. **Transracial and Interracial Adoptees: The Adolescent Years.** Springfield, IL: Thomas, 1983. 155p.

The authors include case studies of interracial adoptions.

McTaggart, Lynn. **The Baby Brokers.** New York: Dial, 1980. 339p.

This in-depth look at marketing babies would be good for a cautious couple to read while considering adoption.

Martin, Cynthia. **Beating the Adoption Game.** La Jolla, CA: Oak Tree Publications, 1980. 304p.

Martin feels artificial insemination, test-tube babies, and surrogate mothers are topics that should be explored in a book on adoption.

Melina, Lois Ruskai. **Adoption: An Annotated Bibliography and Guide.** New York: Garland, 1987. 292p.

A compilation of materials on adoption published since 1974, encompassing issues such as birth parents' rights, preadoption concerns for adoptive parents, special needs adoptions, and search and reunion procedures. A list of children's resources, educational materials, and audiovisual materials is included, as well as an adoption directory by state, a guide to agencies, and a list of organizations.

Merritt, Sharyne, and Linda Steiner. **And Baby Makes Two: Motherhood without Marriage.** New York: Franklin Watts, 1984. 264p.

Case studies and narrative information about unmarried mothers and adoption. Includes bibliographical references.

Musser, Sandra Kay. **I Would Have Searched Forever.** Bala Cynwyd, PA: Jan Enterprises, 1979. 149p.

The author searches for her natural parents.

Nelson, Katherine A. **On the Frontier of Adoption: A Study of Special Needs Adoptive Families.** Washington, DC: Child Welfare League of America, 1985. 110p.

Results of a study that updated and broadened the knowledge of families who adopt children with special needs. Special needs children are defined. The study includes 257 children adopted by 177 families.

Nickman, Steven L. **The Adoption Experience, Stories and Commentaries.** New York: Messner, 1985. 192p.

This book is written for adolescents who are curious about the adoption experience, perhaps because they or their friends are adopted. Through six stories about adopted children and the story of a young man and woman who are the parents of a baby to be adopted, the author conveys both feelings and information about adoption.

Phillips, Maxine. **Adopting a Child.** New York: Public Affairs Committee, 1980. 29p.

Includes a list of organizations involved with adoptions.

Plumez, Jacqueline Hornor. **Successful Adoptions.** New York: Harmony Books, 1982. 234p.

This author devotes space to "Finding Your Child" and "Raising Your Child," and advocates better cooperation among professionals in the field.

Powledge, Fred. **The New Adoption Maze and How To Get through It.** St. Louis, MO: C. V. Mosby, 1985. 322p.

Incorporating new procedures and agency regulations, the author guides the prospective parents on how to make it through the adoption process.

————. **So You're Adopted.** New York: Scribner, 1982. 101p.

Examines the personal concerns and questions that sometimes trouble adopted youngsters and their families; also discusses the social and legal aspects of adoption.

Richards, Arlene, and Irene Willis. **What To Do If You or Someone You Know Is under 18 and Pregnant.** Drawings by Larry Stein, photographs by G. Douglas Thayer. New York: Lothrop, Lee & Shepard, 1983. 256p.

Advice and information for the pregnant teenager on sex, birth control, pregnancy, childbirth, abortion, adoption, marriage, and babies.

Rillera, Mary Jo. **The Adoption Searchbook.** Westminster, CA: Triadoption Publications, 1985. 205p.

Techniques for tracing people are discussed, with a focus on locating natural parents.

Simon, Rita James, and Howard Altstein. **Transracial Adoption.** New York: Wiley, 1977. 197p.

The authors focus on Indian, Afro-American, and Oriental children and their identity in adoptive situations.

Smith, Dorothy W., and Laurie Nehls Sherwen. **Mothers and Their Adopted Children: The Bonding Process.** New York: Tiresias Press, 1983. 160p.

The authors explore mother-child relationships and maternal behavior.

Sorosky, Arthur D., Annette Baran, and Reuben Pannor. **The Adoption Triangle: Sealed or Opened Records, How They Affect Adoptees, Birth Parents, and Adoptive Parents.** Garden City, NY: Anchor Books, 1984. 237p.

This book presents case studies and discussion of right to privacy and right-to-know issues.

Triseliotis, John. **In Search of Origins: The Experiences of Adopted People.** London: Routledge and Kegan Paul, 1973. 177p.

The author based this book on interviews with 70 adoptees who sought information on their birth parents in Scotland as a result of the change in disclosure laws. The kind of information adopted children receive about their backgrounds, the degree of satisfaction with this information, and expectations on the part of adoptees who meet their birth parents are all discussed.

Van Why, Elizabeth Wharton. **Adoption Bibliography and Multi-Ethnic Sourcebook.** Hartford, CT: Open Door Society of Connecticut, 1977. 320p.

This book focuses on children of minorities adopted in the United States.

Viguers, Susan T. **With Child: One Couple's Journey to Their Adopted Children.** San Diego: Harcourt Brace Jovanovich, 1986. 226p.

Using their own experiences, the author relates the adoption process she and her husband went through (an "emotional adventure") as they decided on foreign adoption in the United States.

Will, Reni L., and Jeannine Masterson Michael. **Mom, I'm Pregnant.** Briarcliff Manor, NY: Stein and Day, 1982. 239p.

Discusses the emotional and physical consequences of an unexpected and unwanted pregnancy and explores the various decisions a pregnant girl can make, from abortion to marriage to adoption to keeping the baby.

Wishard, Laurie, and William Wishard. **Adoption: The Grafted Tree.** San Francisco: Cragmont Publications, 1979. 197p.

This guide is written by an adopted daughter and her adoptive father. It attempts to answer questions in a factual, nonemotional style.

ARTICLES

Hunner, Robert J. **"Defining Active and Reasonable Efforts To Preserve Families,"** *Children Today* 15 (November/December 1986): 27–30.

This article focuses on the Indian Child Welfare Act of 1978 and the expectations and results of people working with the Act.

Lord, Lewis J., et al. **"Desperately Seeking Baby,"** *U.S. News & World Report* 103, no. 14 (5 October 1987): 58–64.

A discussion of the desperate attempts infertile couples make to have children and the costs involved.

Ratterman, Debra. **"Judicial Determination of Reasonable Efforts,"** *Children Today* 15 (November/December 1986): 26–31.

A trend in current child welfare practice is the emphasis on improving services so that children may remain in their own homes rather than being placed in foster care. This article reports on preliminary findings of a study dealing with this policy.

Sharp, Pat Tipton. **"Adoption Books over Two Decades,"** *Top of the News* 38, no. 2 (Winter 1982): 151–154.

The article contains a critique of books about adoption written for children and adolescents. The author concludes that books on both levels have given an unrealistic view of adoption and that there is a need for books on adoption that reflect reality and provide accurate information.

Nonprint Materials on Adoption

Cipher in the Snow

Type:	16mm film
Length:	24 min.
Cost:	Rental $15.50
Distributor:	Brigham Young University Media Marketing Provo, UT 84602
Date:	1973

After an eighth-grade boy dies in the snow, an investigation reveals he came from a broken home, was never legally adopted, and was totally ignored by his family, schoolmates, and teachers.

Home from Far

Type:	1/2″ VHS video
Length:	25 min.
Cost:	Rental $12
Distributor:	Atlantis Productions Inc. 1252 La Granada Drive Thousand Oaks, CA 91360
Date:	1984

After the death of her twin brother, Jennie's parents bring two foster children into their home. Jennie resents the boy, Mike, and makes no secret of her hostility. From the Live and Learn Series.

I Don't Know Who I Am

Type:	16mm film, 3/4" or 1/2" video
Length:	30 min.
Cost:	Rental $16
Distributor:	Time-Life Films, Inc.
	Time & Life Building
	1271 Avenue of the Americas
	New York, NY 10020
Date:	1980

For her 16th birthday, Annie Armstrong asks her adoptive parents to help her find her real parents. The film shows the steps involved in her search, which provides her with answers about the real meaning of family. From the series The Teenage Years.

May's Miracle

Type:	16mm film
Length:	28 min.
Cost:	Rental $16.50
Distributor:	Filmmaker's Library Inc.
	133 E. Annapolis Street
	St. Paul, MN 55118
Date:	1982

Severely handicapped at birth, an adopted boy still could not feed himself, stand alone, or speak at 16, in spite of patient care by his adoptive mother May. The miracle is his unexplainable talent as a pianist.

The Pinballs (in two parts)

Type:	16mm film
Length:	31 min.
Cost:	Rental $12
Distributor:	Walt Disney Educational Media Co.
	500 S. Buena Vista Street
	Burbank, CA 91521
Date:	1978

Tells the story of three lonely foster children who learn to care about themselves and about each other. Also available as a two-part filmstrip/cassette presentation.

Superfluous People

Type:	16mm film, 2 reels
Length:	27 min. each
Cost:	Rental $10.50 each

Distributor: Cashier's Office
University of Missouri
123 Jesse Hall
Columbia, MO 65211
Date: 1962

Based on interviews, this film argues that welfare aid is a material and moral problem. A variety of "superfluous people" (babies awaiting adoption, teenage dropouts, displaced elderly) are the subject of the film.

Young, Single and Pregnant
Type: 16mm film
Length: 18 min.
Cost: Rental $10.50
Distributor: Perennial Education Inc.
930 Pitner
Evanston, IL 60202
Date: 1975

Documentary of four young women and their solutions to pregnancy: adoption, abortion, marriage, and single parenthood.

What Happens Now?
Type: Video
Length: 75 min.
Cost: Purchase $145.00
Distributor: Ikongraphics
807 E. Gray
Louisville, KY 40204
Date: 1985

The program examines situations created and questions raised by unwanted teenage pregnancy and discusses the adoption process.

Wild Horses, Broken Wings
Type: 16mm film, 3/4" or 1/2" video
Length: 30 min. or 58 min. in all types
Cost: Purchase $450 (30-min. film), $650 (58-min. film); purchase $250 (30-min. video, either format), $270 (58-min. video, either format)
Distributor: Coronet MTI Film and Video
108 Wilmot Road
Deerfield, IL 60015
Date: 1979

Available in a full-length or a shortened version, *Wild Horses, Broken Wings* tells the story of Davene Bennett, who opened her home and heart to foster children of all races and ages.

Organizations Concerned with Adoption

Agencies are available for would-be parents in their search for a child to adopt, for pregnant women and teenagers who want to investigate the possibility of relinquishing their children, and for adoptees who want to find their birth parents. Other organizations include support and therapy groups.

Adoption Triangle Ministries (ATM)
P.O. Box 1860
Cape Coral, FL 33910
(813) 542-1342
President: Sandra Musser Smith

ATM is for adoptees, adoptive parents, and birth parents (known as the triangle) seeking to work with social workers, clergy, legislators, and others interested in post-adoptive services and in making adoption a more humane institution.

PUBLICATIONS: *List of Networking Organizations* (semiannual), plus occasional tracts and books.

ALMA Society—Adoptees' Liberty Movement Association
P.O. Box 154
Washington Bridge Station
New York, NY 10033
(212) 581-1568
Founder and President: Florence Anna Fisher

ALMA Society was organized in 1971, primarily to help natural parents search for their children and adoptees search for their natural parents. Also organizes support groups to help adoptive parents understand their adopted child's need to search.

Committee for Single Adoptive Parents
P.O. Box 15084
Chevy Chase, MD 20815
(202) 966-6367
Executive Director: Hope Marindin

Single persons who have adopted or wish to adopt children may receive information and assistance from the committee, which supports adoption of children of any race, creed, color, religion, or national origin, as well as handicapped children.

PUBLICATIONS: *Source List* (biennial with 3 updates), *Handbook for Single Adoptive Parents.*

CUB (Concerned United Birthparents)
2000 Walker Street
Des Moines, IA 50317
(319) 359-4068
President: Carole J. Anderson

Organized as a support/advocacy group for birth parents and others interested in adoption reform. Provides "informed choice" for women considering releasing a child for adoption. CUB meets monthly and sponsors a speakers' bureau.

PUBLICATIONS: *Communicator* newsletter (monthly); also publishes pamphlets on "Understanding the Birthparent," "The Birthparent's Perspective," "Choices," "Changes," and "Living as a Birthparent."

Families Adopting Children Everywhere
P.O. Box 28058
Northwood Station
Baltimore, MD 21239
(301) 488-2656
Contact: Laurel Strassberger

Provides support to adoptive parents and families and disseminates information concerning adoption. Sponsors an educational course for prospective adoptive parents.

International Concerns Committee for Children
911 Cypress Drive
Boulder, CO 80303
(303) 494-8333
Treasurer: AnnaMarie Merrill

Helps those interested in adopting children from foreign countries. Provides personal counseling by adoptive parents, and maintains an information and listing service for foreign children in the United States whose adoptions have been disrupted and who need new adoptive parents. Not a child placement agency.

PUBLICATIONS: *Listing Service* (monthly), newsletter (monthly), *Report on Foreign Adoptions* (annual).

International Soundex Reunion Registry
P.O. Box 2312
Carson City, NV 89702
(702) 882-6270
Executive Director: Emma May Vilardi

A service to help adopted or orphaned people (18 or older) find their next-of-kin by birth. The registry also seeks to provide medical and genetic data to registrants. The information is confidential.

PUBLICATION: Newsletter (annual).

Liberal Education for Adoptive Families
23247 Lofton Court
North Scandia, MN 55073
(612) 636-7031
Director: Cheryl Hall

A post-adoption service organization providing legislative and agency policy reform, client counseling, search assistance and referrals, and training for public and private agencies.

National Adoption Exchange
1218 Chestnut Street
Philadelphia, PA 19107
(215) 925-0200
Director: Marlene Piasecki

Serves as an adoption referral service for adoptive parents seeking children with special needs, including older, handicapped, and minority children, and siblings who seek to be placed together.

PUBLICATIONS: Newsletter (quarterly), *Photolisting* (quarterly).

National Coalition to End Racism in America's Child Care System
22075 Koths
Taylor, MI 48180
(313) 295-0257
President: Carol Coccia

Encourages recruitment of foster and adoptive homes of all races and cultures, with the belief that children should not be moved after initial placement just to match their race or culture.

PUBLICATION: *The Children's Voice* (quarterly newsletter).

National Committee for Adoption
P.O. Box 33366
Washington, DC 20033
(202) 638-0469
President: William L. Pierce

Works to protect the institution of adoption, including trying to eliminate nonagency adoptions and ensure the confidentiality of all involved in the adoption process.

PUBLICATIONS: *Memo* (semimonthly), *National Adoption Reports* (bimonthly), *Directory of Resources* (annual), *Unmarried Parents Today* (irregular).

Operation Identity
13101 Blackstone Road NE
Albuquerque, NM 87111
(505) 293-3144
Coordinator: Sally File

Helps individuals 18 or older to search for their families after separation resulting from adoption or divorce. Offers emotional support for the adoptees, adoptive parents, and birthparents.

PUBLICATION: *Operation Identity Newsletter* (quarterly).

Organized Adoption Search Information Services
P.O. Box 53-0761
Miami Shores, FL 33153
(305) 945-2758
Director: Rachel S. Rivers

A search agency that offers assistance for adult adoptees, birth and adoptive parents, orphans, foster children, grandparents of adoptees, and foundlings. Maintains confidential files for each searching member, as well as a registry of birth dates.

Origins
P.O. Box 444
East Brunswick, NJ 08816
(201) 390-4275
Corresponding Secretary: Kathrine Loewenberg

Works particularly with emotional needs of women who have given up their children for adoption. Also arranges for teenage pen pals to provide emotional support for each other.

Orphan Voyage
Cedaredge, CO 81413
(303) 856-3937
Coordinator: Jean M. Paton

Assists in building relationships between adopted people and their kin families, offers support and information to surrendering natural parents, and maintains a library by and about orphans.

PUBLICATIONS: *The Adoption Series* (2 or 3/year), *The Adopted Break Silence*, *Orphan Voyage*.

Ours, Inc.
3307 Highway 100 North, Suite 203
Minneapolis, MN 55422
(615) 535-4829
Executive Director: Susan Frivalds

Offers material and financial support to children seeking permanent placement with a family as well as support for prospective adoptive families. Seeks to create opportunities for successful adoptive placement.

PUBLICATION: *Ours Magazine* (bimonthly).

Parenthesis Adoptive Adolescent Program
P.O. Box 02265
Columbus, OH 43202
(614) 236-2211
Program Coordinator: Judy Emig

Provides post-adoption services, support, and networking for troubled kids and their adoptive parents to aid in communication and problem-solving.

Reunite Inc.
P.O. Box 694
Reynoldsburg, OH 43068
(614) 861-2584
President: Kathy Singer

Assists in adoptee (after age 18) and birthparent searches and encourages legislative adoption reform.

Waif
67 Irving Place
New York, NY 10003
(212) 533-2558
Executive Director: Gerald H. Cornez

Operating on the principle of "a permanent and loving family for every child," the organization raises funds for national and local adoption and advocacy programs.

PUBLICATION: *FYI* newsletter (semiannual).

Yesterday's Children
P.O. Box 1554
Evanston, IL 60204
(312) 545-6900
President: Donna Cullom

Seeks to amend state laws concerning adoption record information in the belief that every adult has a right to his or her historical past.

Hotlines

Almost every urban area has agencies run by the county or state as well as private agencies, often church-related, that are able to help all parties involved with adoption. Consult the telephone directory for your area. The following national numbers are available on a 24-hour basis:

Bethany Christian Services: 1-800-238-4269

Birth Hope Adoption Agency: 1-800-392-2121

National Adoption Hotline: 202-328-1200 (Pregnant women may call collect.)

Southwest Maternity Center: 1-800-255-9612

CHAPTER 7

Finances and the Family

Back at school Angela began to do a lot of probing and self-analysis . . . perhaps she was the one who was being intimidated by the wealth surrounding her. A person didn't have to be rich to be a snob.

Did she dislike these rich kids because they had what she did not? And did they make her feel inferior? She was the same person she had always been.

Hila Colman, *The Double Life of Angela Jones*
(New York: Morrow, 1988), 131.

It is difficult for Angela to be objective about her relationships at school when she contrasts her poor family background with those of the wealthy students around her. Material possessions should not be the yardstick by which people measure others. Unfortunately, in our society people are often judged more for what they have than who they are.

Family finances differ as much as family structure. Father is the sole source of income for some families, Mother for others. Many families today have both parents working, while some families are on welfare. Some families invest their money in real estate, stocks, or bonds, while others have savings accounts, and still others have nothing to invest. Some families buy many things on credit, others abhor the idea.

Finances play an important role in the well-being of the family. If families discuss their finances and allow younger members to help with decisions, young people will have a better understanding of what expectations are reasonable. Adolescents, in particular, can be an asset to managing family finances. If adolescents have no knowledge of income or expenses, they can not be full participants in family decisions.

Terms

Allowance. Money that a family income-earner gives to those who are underage but who need the experience of handling their own money; the amount usually increases as a child grows older and/or more responsible. Some allowances are a set, agreed-upon amount per week or month, while others are "on demand" as need arises.

Budget. Planning by an individual or family whereby the expenses for a period are adjusted or scheduled according to the estimated or fixed income for that period.

Inflation. Occurs when the value of money falls and prices go up. Inflation has a negative effect on buying power, since a dollar of income will not buy the same quantity of goods it did in the past.

Family Income

Although family income has increased in the last two decades, inflation has diminished the buying power of the dollar.

- In 1973, the average 30-year-old earned $23,500 in inflation-adjusted dollars, which declined 25 percent in purchasing power to $17,520 by 1983 (*AFL-CIO News*, 7).
- Average family income in this age group fell 14 percent during the 1973 to 1983 decade, despite a large increase in two-earner households (ibid.).
- To purchase a median-priced home in 1973, the average 30-year-old spent 21 percent of gross monthly earnings on mortgage payments, contrasted with 44 percent by 1983 (ibid.).

Single-parent households, especially those headed by women (the majority) fared considerably worse than two-parent families. The average pretax income for a female-headed family in 1985 was $15,264, compared with an average of $36,847 for married couple families with children (ibid.).

In 1986, 13.6 percent of the total population was living below the poverty level. The percentages were dramatically higher for black people, of whom 31.1 percent fell below the poverty line, and for Hispanics, 27.3 percent of whom were poor. Millions more have incomes only marginally higher than poverty level. In 1987, 21 percent of all children under 16 were living in poverty, most of them in single-parent homes (*Statistical Abstract, 1988,* 433).

Family Expenses

Before groceries, clothing, or luxuries such as movie tickets, video-cassette recorders and vacations can be purchased, there are a number of claims made on the family income. Each family has a variety of fixed and variable expenses which must be paid on a regular basis. These include taxes, rent or mortgage payments, utilities, and insurance.

TAXES

As an old saying goes, "Nothing's certain but death and taxes." The amount of taxes a family pays has a strong impact on how much money the family actually has to spend. And the amount paid out in taxes has to do with the tax structures of the nation, state, and community where each family resides. Taxes provide the revenue needed to support government services most people take for granted, such as schools, police and fire protection, libraries, road construction and maintenance, social services, and the legal system, to name just a few.

The three main types of taxes are income taxes, sales taxes, and property taxes.

Income taxes. These are paid to the federal and most state governments and are usually calculated as a percentage of income received. The percentage of family income paid in taxes varies with the amount earned and the deductions that are allowed. Federal tax rates are set by Congress, and state tax rates are set by each individual state legislature. Taxes are collected on an annual basis by the Internal Revenue Service (IRS) and individual state revenue services.

Penalties for fraud or failure to pay income taxes can be severe. Each year, the Internal Revenue Service selects returns for auditing. Some returns are selected because something seems suspicious, or because of certain factors like high deductions for business expenses or charitable deductions. A certain percentage of returns are selected at random. If the audit shows that income was underreported or that some deductions are not allowable, the taxpayer may have to pay more tax, plus interest and penalties.

Sales taxes. In addition to state income tax, most states collect sales tax on items purchased within the state. Sales taxes are also collected by cities, counties, and special districts set up to provide services like fire protection or recreational facilities. The sales tax is a percentage of the price of goods or services that is added to the cost of the item at the time of sale. Merchants collect sales taxes when they sell a product or service, then pass the revenue on to the various government bodies.

Property taxes. Property taxes are levied on real estate by local communities. The property tax is based on the assessed value of a piece of property as compared to the values of other homes and businesses in the area. Although only property owners pay property tax, the cost of paying the tax is usually incorporated into the amount charged for renting a piece of property such as a house or apartment.

MORTGAGES, UTILITIES, HEALTH CARE, INSURANCE

Besides taxes, families have other regular expenses to consider when they plan their budgets. There are rent or mortgage payments for the house or apartment, along with bills for utilities such as electricity, heating and air-conditioning, water, sewer, and trash collection. Most people have a telephone, which requires payment of a monthly bill. Automobile or other loan payments, credit card charges, and special expenses such as child care are also regular expense items in many budgets.

Insurance is another major expense. Insurance companies collect regular premiums in exchange for a commitment to pay unexpected expenses that arise as the result of accidents, fires, illness, or death. Most states require car owners to carry insurance on their automobiles. Many families also insure their houses, businesses, and personal property such as furniture, television sets, clothing, and jewelry. Income-earners may also choose to purchase life insurance, which will help provide for their dependents in case they are disabled or die.

Families that do not have health insurance through a parent's employer must find other ways to pay for medical coverage. The cost of health care has been increasing at a rapid rate and the premiums for such insurance have become very high, especially for people who are insured as individuals rather than through a group policy.

Besides the basic expenses described above, different families have different priorities for spending their money. One family might consider cable television a necessity. Another family might be saving for a vacation.

Dual-Income Families

The needs described above, combined with a desire for a variety of material possessions and the effects of inflation, means that many families cannot get by on a single income. As a result, in an increasing number of families both parents work at income-producing jobs. In 1986, 55 percent of all women in married couple families were in the paid work force (*Statistical Abstract, 1988,* 373).

Many mothers work only part-time to "help out" on expenses or so the family can afford extras. Other women find it necessary to work full-time to meet the family's expenses. And some women, dissatisfied with jobs that pay an hourly wage, have decided they want careers that pay them salaries as well as providing for more personal growth. Such a decision usually requires more education and a greater commitment in time and energy.

Many changes have become apparent in our society as a result of the number of women working. Requests for day-care facilities for young children have increased dramatically. A few businesses have begun to provide maternity leave and day care for children of employees, but for most working parents finding good, affordable child care remains a persistent problem.

Some schools have found it more difficult to communicate with parents when no one is home during the day. Parent conferences have to be held at different hours so parents can attend, and discipline problems or health crises at school may have to be resolved in ways other than a telephone call to the parents.

Many children in two-income families have had to learn independence early, since they are alone so much. They have to take care of themselves, often performing chores around the house as part of their routine before the parents come home. Recognizing the problems of "latch-key" children who have no one to go home to at the end of the school day, some schools have instituted after-school programs to keep children busy and supervised until parents can pick them up after work.

Teenagers are playing an increasingly adult role in today's families because of the increase in working mothers. Seventy percent of teens have working mothers and half of their mothers work full-time (Hauser, 38). One effect of dual-income families is that young people are increasingly responsible for the family shopping. In *American Demographics*, Grady Hauser notes that teenagers spend more money on their families than they spend on themselves (ibid.). Most of that spending is done in grocery stores. Teenagers and children also have considerable influence on family purchases such as video and electronic equipment, clothing, and vacations. In addition, Hauser notes that:

- Girls 16 and 17 years old spend more of their families' income than boys because they grocery shop more often (ibid.)
- Fifty-two percent of girls aged 12 to 19 shop for part or all of the family's groceries each week (ibid.).
- While older girls grocery shop almost two hours each week on average, younger girls shop one hour and 45 minutes a week and boys average about 45 minutes weekly (ibid., 40).
- Eighty-five percent of teenagers who do the family grocery shopping say they shop at a large supermarket where a full range of brands is available (ibid.).

Older teenage shoppers are more likely to make brand choices than younger ones, a fact recognized by many advertisers. Brand loyalties formed during the teenage years can last a lifetime (ibid.). Advertising between songs on rock videos or on teen-targeted television programs is a common tactic of companies that seek to establish such loyalties among young shoppers.

Teenagers can do more of the family shopping because they are more independent than they used to be. Many of them have cars and a job. One in four teenagers owns a new or used car; among boys aged 18 and 19, 61 percent own a car. Forty-four percent of teenagers have a full- or part-time job in the summer. Among 18- and 19-year-olds, over 83 percent have full- or part-time summer jobs (ibid.). Most teenagers who work do not contribute any of their earnings to their families.

Another indicator of the independence of today's teenagers is their use of various forms of credit. Thirty-four percent of teenagers bought by direct mail in the past year. Twelve percent have access to a credit card. Credit card ownership or access rises to 35 percent among 18- to 19-year old girls.

Credit card use by teenagers is directly correlated with family income. Teenagers living in suburban households with annual incomes of $50,000 or more have a credit card use index of 188 (with 100 being average), while teens from lower-income rural homes are indexed at 36 (ibid.). Of the 3.5 million teenagers who have access to a credit card, 60 percent are girls aged 15 to 19. The major categories of credit card expenditures for these girls are clothing, health, and beauty aids. Seventy-six percent of teenage girls buy their own brand of toothpaste, and over 65 percent buy eye makeup (ibid.).

Saving for College

Many families are concerned about being able to pay for their children's college educations, but most young people are not saving money for college themselves. A Gallup poll conducted in August and September of 1988, based on telephone interviews of 1,001 people between the ages of 13 and 21, indicated that fewer than six out of ten young people have saved for their college education. Nearly 50 percent said tuition costs prevent many from seeking a higher education, but claimed they would get loans (37 percent), look for a part-time job (32 percent), or select another college (14 percent). Fifty-nine percent of high school juniors and seniors polled said they or someone in their families had saved for their college education. The rest said they didn't know (Associated Press).

REFERENCES

"American Dream Fades for Post-War Generation," *AFL-CIO News* 31, no. 2 (11 January 1986): 7.

Associated Press. "Poll Shows Many Teens Aren't Saving for College," *Boulder Daily Camera*, 10 October 1988.

Cole, Sheila. *Working Kids on Working*. New York: Lothrop, Lee & Shepard, 1980.

Colman, Hila. *The Double Life of Angela Jones*. New York: Morrow, 1988.

Hauser, Grady. "How Teenagers Spend Money: The Family Dollar," *American Demographics* 8, no. 12 (December 1986): 38–41.

Statistical Abstract of the United States, 1988: National Data Book and Guide to Sources, 108th edition. Washington, DC: Government Printing Office, 1987.

Resources
for Finding Out about Family Finances

Fiction about Family Finances

Bates, Betty. **My Mom, the Money Nut.** New York: Holiday House, 1979. 158p.

Fritzi, an eighth grader whose dad is one of the few in her new school who works with his hands instead of at a desk, is uncomfortable that her mother is so interested in money and wants to talk about it all the time. When Fritzi visits her grandfather, she gains insight into her mother's behavior and comes to terms with her resentment.

Colman, Hila. **The Double Life of Angela Jones.** New York: Morrow, 1988. 156p.

After growing up in a poor neighborhood in New York, Angela Jones receives a scholarship to an exclusive school in New Hampshire. The wealth and pretensions there irritate her until she meets Andy, a boy from town whom she likes. Angela has to decide whether she will live the lie that she is wealthy and deceive Andy or be truthful and keep her self-respect.

Klass, Sheila Solomon. **Credit-Card Carole.** New York: Scribner's, 1987. 137p.

Carole's dad, a conservative, normal, successful dentist, decides to give it all up and seek his career with his first love, the stage. The family income changes drastically and Carole's shopping trips to the mall are curtailed. But Carole learns that the bond of love and closeness in the family is a value money can't buy.

Shyer, Marlene Fanta. **Adorable Sunday.** New York: Scribner's, 1983. 182p.

Sunday Donaldson's mother is obsessed with getting "adorable" eighth grader Sunday into a modeling career, almost at the expense of her happy family. Sunday is the one who realizes that the money and fame were bought at too high a price.

Tolan, Stephanie S. **The Great Skinner Strike.** New York: Macmillan, 1983. 112p.

Considering itself middle-class, the Skinner family consists of four children, a father who is a middle-level executive in a small company, and a mother who is a part-time research librarian. Mother goes on a one-person strike and the family has to reassess its priorities.

———. **The Great Skinner Enterprise.** New York: Macmillan, 1986. 175p.

In this sequel to *The Great Skinner Strike*, conservative Mr. Skinner begins to change: he gets fired, buys an expensive van and starts a family business designed to do errands and odd jobs for busy people. The entire family gets involved in a chaotic enterprise that almost destroys them.

Nonfiction Materials on Family Finances

BOOKS

Cole, Sheila. *Working Kids on Working.* New York: Lothrop, Lee & Shepard, 1980. 219p.

The author recorded and summarized interviews with 25 young people who discussed their work experiences. Information on child labor laws and legal information on working minors is included.

Fitzgibbon, Dan. **All about Your Money.** Decorations by David Marshall. New York: Atheneum, 1984. 135p.

With a light but sensible approach, the author introduces young readers to money management, use of credit cards, and the job market for young people. The question of where to keep your money and attitudes toward money are two of fourteen topics touched on in the book.

Kyte, Kathy S. **The Kids' Complete Guide to Money.** Drawings by Richard Brown. New York: Knopf, 1984. 89p.

A guide to making one's money supply go as far as possible through sensible spending as well as creative bartering, borrowing, swapping, and sharing. Free and inexpensive entertainment opportunities are also discussed.

Lasker, Joe. **Mothers Can Do Anything.** Chicago: Albert Whitman, 1972. 37p.

A picture book showing mothers in a variety of occupations.

Mitchell, Joyce Slayton. **My Mommy Makes Money.** Illustrated by True Kelley. Boston: Little, Brown, 1984. 31p.

A picture book depicting mother as a provider in the home.

Morgan, Tom. **Money, Money, Money: How To Get and Keep It.** Illustrations by Joe Ciardiello. New York: Putnam's, 1978. 118p.

A Junior Literary Guild selection, this book contains down-to-earth advice for young people about how they can make and lose money. Chapters include topics such as gambling, borrowing, inflation, and bankruptcy.

ARTICLE

Hauser, Grady. **"How Teenagers Spend the Family Dollar,"** *American Demographics* 8, no. 12 (December 1986): 38–41.

Stating that today's teenagers spend more of the family dollar as they take on increased responsibility in the family, the author analyzes the source of the money teens spend, how they spend it, and effects of advertising on teens as consumers.

Nonprint Materials on Family Finances

Adolescent Responsibilities: Craig and Mark

Type:	16mm film
Length:	28 min.
Cost:	Rental $13.50
Distributor:	Cashier's Office
	University of Missouri
	123 Jesse Hall
	Columbia, MO 65211
Date:	1973

Craig and Mark are teenage brothers struggling for independence and their own values. Their family's decision to move raises questions about work and money, responsibilities and privileges.

Cornell Family Matters

Type:	16mm film or video
Length:	30 min.
Cost:	Purchase $336 (film); rental $14, purchase $150 (video)
Distributor:	Cornell University
	A-V Resource Center, Media Services
	8 Research Park
	Ithaca, NY 14850
Date:	1984

Two families with similar situations fare differently—a black single-parent family and a white family with both parents working.

Families Get Angry

Type:	Various video formats
Length:	9 min.
Cost:	Purchase, no amount indicated
Distributor:	AIMS Media
	6901 Woodley Avenue
	Van Nuys, CA 91406-4878
Date:	1972

After a family quarrel over financial difficulties, a boy attempts to analyze and deal with his problems.

Left Out

Type:	Film or video
Length:	24 min.
Cost:	Rental $50, purchase $495 (film); purchase $395 (video)
Distributor:	AIMS Media
	6901 Woodley Avenue
	Van Nuys, CA 91406-4878
Date:	1987

An embarrassed and disappointed Amy, age 12, cannot afford the expense of a class trip because her father is unemployed. Amy feels put upon and isolated from the fun, but she finally realizes that it is her father who feels worse pain.

CHAPTER 8

Divorce and the Children of Divorce

"It wasn't the worst time when Melody left me," the Professor said. "The worst time was years before. Because I didn't know I could hate anybody that much, I didn't know I could be that angry, I didn't know what to do except concentrate on my work. I didn't know anybody could hurt anybody else that much; it was like she'd stuck a sword into me, one of those Japanese samurai swords . . . heavy and razor sharp—and curved—and she'd stuck it in me and then she was . . . pushing it around. . . . When I found out how many lies she was telling me, I finally realized that she had always lied to me . . . I didn't think she'd do that to you, Jeff. But she did, didn't she?"
> Cynthia Voigt, A Solitary Blue (New York: Macmillan, 1983), 100.

Jeff was only in second grade when his mother, Melody, deserted him and his professor father. For years, Jeff doesn't know what happened or why, but he is sure he was the reason. He knows his parents are divorced now, but fearing his father will leave him too, Jeff tries hard not to interrupt the Professor while he works and thinks only of pleasing him.

Divorce in the United States Today

Much has been written about the rise in divorce rates through the years. Analysis of Census Bureau statistics in 1987 indicated that the two-decade-long increase in divorces seems to have stopped its climb (Norton and Moorman, 4). In the 1970s, nearly one of every two marriages ended in divorce. In the 1980s, the divorce rate seems to be leveling off (ibid.).

- The proportion of women in their twenties who are divorced increased from 1975 to 1980, but did not change significantly from 1980 to 1985 (ibid., 5).
- Women who wait until they are 30 or older to marry tend to have more stable marriages over the long run (ibid., 12).
- Divorce was most likely for women who first marry while still in their teens and for those who give birth within seven months after being married. Divorce is also higher among women with incomplete educations (ibid.).
- At least 60 percent of all divorces involve children (ibid., 11).
- Seventy-five percent of women who divorce ultimately remarry (ibid., 13).

Terms

Coparenting. Describes the relationship of a divorced couple who continue to share the care of and concern for their common children. Coparenting arrangements often involve stepfamilies and a parent and children who do not live in the same home (Keshet, 19).

Custody. Having responsibility for and authority over a minor.

Children and Divorce

Children are considered the victims in divorce. They may bear emotional scars from living in a home filled with fighting and tension. While they may realize their parents are fighting and unhappy, most children do not think in terms of something as final as divorce. When the divorce happens, they may carry guilt and resentment around with them for years. Often they have a sense of shame and personal failure and express embarrassment at their parents' divorce. Teenagers have admitted they didn't want friends around for fear they would find out about their parents' divorce.

The feeling of embarrassment is a reaction to the fact that most children will instinctively try to keep their parents together, and then feel ashamed when their attempts fail. Studies have found, however, that many young people felt divorce was the only solution to their family problems. Many were relieved that some solution had been found. Even through the relief, however, they felt resentment, bitterness, and hurt.

Children may display long-term effects from their parents' divorce. Some young married people have said their own marriages suffered because they find it difficult to establish trust with a marriage partner. They may have a deep-seated fear of failure in their own marriage.

In a study that compared 703 adult children of divorce on eight measures of psychological well-being with 1,042 persons who had experienced the death of a parent before age 16 and 7,954 persons who were living with both natural parents at age 16, Norval Glenn found the adult children of divorce compared unfavorably with the other groups on almost all of the measures of well-being. Females were lower than women from intact families by a significant margin on six of the eight measures, the men on three (Glenn, 68).

FIGHTING AND SEPARATION

In The Kids' Book of Divorce, children said they recognized the signs of parental fighting: "voices rising, becoming harsher and more shrill, eyes narrowing, bodies becoming tense; people throwing things; slamming doors; someone not paying attention or ignoring another person" (Rofes, 8). The children felt fear, anger, embarrassment, disappointment, or insecurity when their parents fought. Sometimes parents would ask a child to take sides, which caused even worse problems.

Arguments in a family do not mean serious problems with the marriage. They may help make it more healthy. But if the fights happen all the time and go deeper and deeper, it may be harmful for everyone's mental health for such behavior to continue. This is when a separation is usually suggested.

According to The Kids' Book of Divorce, separation has three major causes: "Parents can't be together in pleasant ways, people expect too much from a marriage, and people expect marriage to be an answer to all their problems, but marriage is not a problem solver" (ibid., 19). The decision to separate can happen suddenly or after long discussions. Sometimes a separation helps the couple see how much they love each other, or it gives them time to work out a particular problem. Some couples use the time to get professional help from a marriage counselor.

Most separations do end in divorce, but the separation can give the entire family a chance to think about how their lives might change. Parents sometimes agree to live together "for the kids' sake," but continued unpleasantness is not beneficial for either children or parents.

It is important for young people to be able to talk about their feelings and have help understanding what is happening. Children and teenagers need to realize they are not the cause of the separation and they should not feel guilty about the difficulty their parents are having.

Evidence of a detrimental effect on school work by "high-conflict families," whether the parents were divorced or not, was the result of a study by Rex Forehand, a psychologist from the University of Georgia. Children were rated by teachers on characteristics such as cognitive abilities, communication skills, and lying or disobedience. The children of high-conflict divorced parents got the lowest score. Teenagers often overtly manifest the damaging effects of divorce— girls tended toward alcohol and drug abuse and boys toward criminal behaviors such as theft and drug pedaling. Even college-age children are vulnerable to the effects of divorce, which can put an added burden on them at a stressful time in their lives.

TELLING THE CHILDREN

The way a divorce is handled makes a difference in how it affects everyone involved. One of the most difficult tasks parents have during a divorce is telling the children. Because it is an emotional and trying time, parents may put this task off until arrangements have been completed. They may say to themselves that they don't want to hurt the children, or they may hate to admit that their marriage has failed. Some parents may be overly casual about this important decision, which confuses the children even more.

Looking back on the experience later, many children say it is the feeling of being left out or of not being important in the decisions that hurt them the most during the divorce. Children who are not warned ahead of time but come home to find one parent abruptly gone find it especially difficult to adjust. Good communications with both parents help to make an awkward situation work out more pleasantly. Parents need to assure the children that they still love them, even if they no longer love each other.

Respondents in a study by Glynnis Walker, who were an average of 11 years old at the time of their parents' divorce and 19 at the time of the study, felt their parents could have done a better job of getting divorced, meaning "They could have talked to us about it."

Some said, "I wish they had done it sooner." Others commented, "They should have been more open about the causes and effects so that we understood better why it was happening." Another said, "They should have been more friendly to each other. I would not say the things they said in front of the children" (Walker, 202).

Support groups for children experiencing divorce are available in some schools and through various agencies. Joining a group lets young people hear how others are handling similar problems and may give ideas for solutions. Such a group provides support when things are not going well, as well as encouragement for trying new approaches. Just knowing others understand one's situation is a boost to sagging spirits. Such groups also give individuals a chance to help others who are in the same or similar situations.

POSSIBLE CUSTODY ARRANGEMENTS

Of the many decisions surrounding divorce, choosing appropriate living arrangements for the children is of crucial importance. The number of alternatives has expanded in recent years. Following are a few of the choices.

Divided or alternating custody. Each parent has sole custody for a period of time. For instance, one parent may take the child during the summer and the other during the school year. Unless the parents agree to make joint decisions, the parent with whom the child is residing at a particular time will govern the situation at that time (ibid., 177).

Joint legal custody. Both parents retain and share the right to legal responsibility for the child, who may actually live with only one parent. Both parents have access to medical or educational records, and both can make decisions about what schools the child attends or what religious training is given. Both parents are responsible if the child causes trouble, either legal or financial (ibid., 178).

Joint physical custody. Both parents share physical custody of the child, but only one has full legal custody. This can be difficult for the parent who has no legal say in much of the child's life, but is expected to share equal responsibility for the child's behavior.

Sole custody. One parent has total control and legal responsibility for the child, even to the point of deciding when, where, how often, and under what circumstances the child is permitted to see the other parent (ibid., 177). It is estimated that custody is not contested in 80 to 90 percent of divorce cases and the mother is granted custody in nine out of ten cases. However, since the late 1970s, more fathers are asking for custody of their children.

Split custody. Some of the children live with one parent and some with another, with appropriate visitation back and forth (ibid.).

Third-party custody. Neither parent chooses or is capable of taking care of the child or children. The court appoints a guardian to take responsibility for the child, finds a relative who will care for the child, or places the child in a home through a public agency (Rofes, 49).

The Uniform Marriage and Divorce Act says that courts should take into consideration "the economic circumstances of each spouse at the time the division of property is to become effective, including the desirability of awarding the family home . . . to the spouse having custody of any children." Furthermore, the financial resources of the custodial parent and the standard of living the child would have enjoyed had the marriage not been dissolved are also factors considered by the court. Federal law now requires states to withhold wages when a parent fails to make court-ordered child support payments after 30 days (Walker, 104).

Child support is not tax deductible to the one who pays it or taxable to the one who receives it. This is a bone of contention with many fathers, who are usually on the paying end of the equation.

The Divorce Process

The divorce process varies from state to state, but usually there is a residency requirement and a specified time for separation, such as living apart for 30 days. One parent has to file a complaint against the other, stating the reason for the divorce, whom they want to get custody and pay child support, and who gets alimony. Parents usually have lawyers handle the details of the divorce for them. Since legal help is often expensive, however, they may go to a legal aid clinic for inexpensive help. The children sometimes meet with the lawyer, too, since part of the lawyer's job is to protect the children's rights.

No-fault divorce has been legalized in many states and is based on "irretrievable breakdown of the marriage." This means that couples can get a divorce if it is obvious that the marriage is falling apart and there is no hope of saving it. The advantage of no-fault divorce is that it lets parents end an unsuccessful marriage without becoming enemies in court. If both parents agree to a no-fault divorce, a dissolution agreement is signed by both parents, and the terms of custody and support are agreed upon (Rofes, 55).

Mediation is an out-of-court divorce agreement worked out between husband and wife with the help of a trained mediator. Both partners are present at the mediation meetings and are encouraged to express their wants and financial needs. The needs of the children are discussed and recommendations are made to the court. The advantage of this system is that the parents are working with trained, professional experts, and creative solutions to problems of custody and visitation may be reached (ibid., 57).

If the mother assumes her maiden name or remarries, her name will then be different from the names of the children. The children's names do not change unless the children are legally adopted by a stepfather or unless they go through the courts to change their name. Such name changes, although not a major problem, can complicate children's lives and cause confusion at school, for example, when teachers do not know how to address a parent.

Research on Children of Divorce

Many social scientists are interested in the effects of divorce on children, but so far it is hard to generalize the results of some of the research because of the small numbers of subjects used. As a result there is considerable disagreement on the long-term effects of divorce on children.

Judith Wallerstein and Joan Kelly, for example, conclude "These youngsters (in the study) taught us a lot about the extended aftermath to the marital disruption: the staying power of feelings . . . reappearing throughout the child's growing up years and perhaps into adulthood as well" (Wallerstein and Kelly, 303).

Glynnis Walker, on the other hand, writes that "children are the ones who manage to handle the divorce best of all. . . . Overall, 74 percent of the respondents (368) said they had a good relationship with at least one of their parents years after the divorce; of that 74 percent, 35 percent said their relationship was good with both parents" (Walker, 205). She believes we are taught divorce is bad, creating a self-fulfilling prophecy. If people believed no good could come of divorce, and anybody who went through it had to suffer and be marked for life by the experience, then that is what happened (ibid., 207).

Young people, the children of divorce, are unique in their situations and their experiences. Researchers are looking for trends and readers must be cautious about taking just one point of view on this emotional and controversial topic.

REFERENCES

Glenn, Norval D. "Children of Divorce," *Psychology Today* 19, no. 6 (June 1985): 68–69.

Keshet, Jamie K. *Love and Power in the Stepfamily: A Practical Guide.* New York: McGraw-Hill, 1987.

Norton, Arthur J., and Jeanne E. Moorman. "Current Trends in Marriage and Divorce among American Women," *Journal of Marriage and the Family* 49, no. 1 (February 1987): 3–14.

Rofes, Eric E., and the students at Fayerweather Street School. *The Kids' Book of Divorce: By, for and about Kids.* Lexington, MA: Lewis Publishing, 1981.

Voigt, Cynthia. *A Solitary Blue.* New York: Macmillan, 1983.

Walker, Glynnis. *Solomon's Children: Exploding the Myths of Divorce.* New York: Arbor House, 1986.

Wallerstein, Judith S., and Joan Berlin Kelly. *Surviving the Breakup: How Children and Parents Cope with Divorce.* New York: Basic Books, 1980.

Resources
for Finding Out about Divorce

Fiction about Divorce

Abercrombie, Barbara Mattes. **Cat-Man's Daughter.** New York: Harper & Row, 1981. 154p.

For two years, 13-year-old Kate has lived in New York with her divorced mother, going several times during the year to Los Angeles to visit her father. She feels like a ping-pong ball, but discovers she has to make the best of what she has.

Adler, C. S. **The Silver Coach.** New York: Coward, McCann, 1979. 122p.

Chris, 12, and her sister Jackie, 7, will live with their father's mother while their mother attends summer school. After father arrives for a visit bringing another woman and her children, Chris and Jackie become less self-centered and more loving under their grandmother's influence.

Angell, Judie. **What's Best for You.** New York: Bradbury, 1981. 187p.

Their parents' recent divorce has Lee, 15, Allison, 12, and Joel, 7, packing, moving, and experiencing mixed emotions. Candid insights into the convictions and misgivings of each family member as each struggles to adapt to the divorce.

Bach, Alice. **A Father Every Few Years.** New York: Harper & Row, 1977. 144p.

Tim feels guilty about both his father's and his stepfather's leaving, and is fearful that his mother will abandon him too.

Blume, Judy. **It's Not the End of the World.** New York: Bradbury Press, 1972. 169p.

Karen, a sixth grade student, can't believe her parents are getting a divorce. She plots to get them together in the same room, believing that will make a difference. She finally realizes they can still love their children though not each other.

Cleary, Beverly. **Dear Mr. Henshaw.** New York: Dell, 1983. 134p.

In this Newbery Award-winning book, Leigh Botts starts writing to an author, Mr. Henshaw, when he is in second grade and lonely because of his parents' divorce. Through his letters, he progresses in acceptance of himself.

Corcoran, Barbara. **Hey, That's My Soul You're Stomping On.** New York: Atheneum, 1978. 144p.

Sent to live with her grandparents while her parents are dealing with their divorce, Rachel finds new friends who have had similar problems and are helpful to her in understanding her problems.

Danziger, Paula. **The Divorce Express.** New York: Dell, 1982. 148p.

Since the divorce, Phoebe lives with her father in Woodstock and commutes to New York City by bus (The Divorce Express) on the weekends to live with her mother. She makes friends with Rosie, whose problems are much like her own.

Goldman, Katie. **In the Wings.** New York: Dial, 1982. 176p.

The pain of her parents' separation and impending divorce affects Jessie's grades, her big part in the school play, and her relationship with her best friend, Andrea, until she accepts the situation.

Grant, Cynthia D. **Joshua Fortune.** New York: Atheneum, 1980. 152p.

Joshua is 14 and his parents were hippies when he was born. Eventually his father, who likes to travel, leaves for good. The mother gets her teaching certificate, the family moves a lot, and Josh has to adjust to his mother's remarriage.

Greene, Constance C. **A Girl Called Al.** New York: Dell, 1977. 128p.

Alexandria, whose parents are divorced, is an overweight seventh grader trying to get her mother's attention while filling up on sweets and acting like she doesn't care about her feelings of rejection.

Gregory, Diana. **The Fog Burns Off by 11 O'Clock.** New York: Addison-Wesley, 1981. 155p.

Thirteen-year-old Dede Applegate comes to terms with growing up and her parent's divorce during a summer vacation spent with her father and his new girlfriend in California.

Holland, Isabelle. **Heads You Win, Tails I Lose.** New York: Lippincott, 1973. 159p.

Melissa is angry about her parents' separating, and remembering all the times they nagged her about her weight, she steals her mother's diet pills.

Irwin, Hadley. **Bring to a Boil and Separate.** New York: Atheneum, 1980. 123p.

Katie, 13, tells about the emotional upheavals divorce brings to her life. Katie feels her parents are divorcing her, although her mother tries to reassure her of both parents' love.

Klein, Norma. **Angel Face.** New York: Viking, 1984. 228p.

At 15, Jason is unprepared for the responsibility of consoling his mother after his father leaves with another woman.

————. **Taking Sides.** New York: Pantheon, 1974. 176p.

Nell and her little brother live with their father. They are confused, since most of their friends whose parents are divorced live with their mothers. Their father's illness changes the situation and adds to their confusion.

Levine, Betty K. **The Great Burgerland Disaster.** New York: Atheneum, 1981. 120p.

A 15-year-old boy who fails to understand the emotions that brought about his parents' divorce tries to find success in the fast-food business.

Love, Sandra Weller. **Crossing Over.** New York: Lothrop, Lee & Shepard, 1981. 155p.

After three years of living with Mother and her belief in independence, Megan and Kevin move in with Father and his belief in structure. Mother goes to graduate school, and Megan finally learns to share feelings with her father.

Meyer, Carolyn. **C.C. Poindexter.** New York: Atheneum, 1978. 216p.

Already six feet tall, C.C. has to cope with her physical appearance and the fact that her parents have divorced. She then has to face her mother's attempts to succeed in business and the possibility of her father's remarriage.

Miklowitz, Gloria. **The Day the Senior Class Got Married.** New York: Dell, 1983. 157p.

Lori and Garrick are part of the senior consumer economics class, which plays the "marriage game," but Lori also has divorced parents who complicate her plans to marry Garrick for real in June.

Miner, Jane Claypool. **Split Decision: Facing Divorce.** Mankato, MN: Crestwood House, 1982. 63p.

Ann's story reveals the painful and powerful drive some children feel to mend their parents' troubled marriage. The focus of the book is on Ann's determination to affect her parents' decision. From the Crisis Series.

Neufeld, John. **Sunday Father.** New York: Signet, 1976. 159p.

Tessa and her younger brother dream of getting their mother and father together again. Their father visits them regularly on Sundays, making it hard for Tessa to believe her father when he announces he is getting married to another woman.

Okimoto, Jean Davies. **My Mother Is Not Married to My Father.** New York: Putnam's, 1979. 109p.

A rather classic case of divorce is seen through the eyes of Cynthia, who narrates the book. The children's responses of denial, guilt, anger, confusion, misplaced hope, regression, bargaining, and finally acceptance and adjustment are all included. Their sensitive mother helps them talk out their feelings.

Platt, Kin. **The Boy Who Could Make Himself Disappear.** New York: Dell, 1971. 224p.

Roger, feeling worthless as a result of an accident when he was a child and his parents' divorce, tries to make himself disappear.

Sallis, Susan. **An Open Mind.** New York: Harper & Row, 1978. 139p.

David, who lives with his mother and sees his father only on weekends, has new conflicts with the spastic son of his father's girlfriend.

Voigt, Cynthia. **A Solitary Blue.** New York: Macmillan, 1983. 189p.

Jeff's mother left home when Jeff was in second grade. He tries to keep his father, the Professor, from being upset. When Jeff is eleven, he visits his mother in South Carolina. Enthralled with her on the first visit, he is totally disillusioned on the second visit.

Wolitzer, Hilma. **Out of Love.** New York: Farrar, Straus & Giroux, 1976. 160p.

Unable to understand how her parents fell out of love, Teddy's hopes that they will be reunited are destroyed when her father remarries and her new stepmother becomes pregnant.

Wood, Phyllis Anderson. **Win Me and You Lose.** New York: New American Library, 1978. 136p.

Given the choice of which parent he will live with following their divorce, 17-year-old Matt chooses his father and they learn to respect each other.

Nonfiction Materials on Divorce

BOOKS

Anderson, Hal W., and Gail S. Anderson. **Mom and Dad Are Divorced, But I'm Not: Parenting after Divorce.** Chicago: Nelson-Hall, 1981. 258p.

Written to help divorcing parents counsel their children, the authors stress being honest without burdening children with too many details of the divorce. Their "down-to-earth" approach includes advice on finances after the divorce is over.

Berger, Stuart. **Divorce without Victims: Helping Children through Divorce with a Minimum of Pain and Trauma.** Boston: Houghton Mifflin, 1983. 200p.

A compassionate survival guide for parents that gives advice and insight into how the child may be experiencing the parents' divorce.

Boeckman, Charles. **Surviving Your Parents' Divorce.** New York: Franklin Watts, 1980. 133p.

Written for young people, this book contains a range of topics: a child's feelings about parental fights and abuse, guilt and fear, and understanding divorce proceedings. Includes a resource list for advice.

Bohannan, Paul. **All the Happy Families: Exploring the Varieties of Family Life.** New York: McGraw-Hill, 1985. 262p.

The author has divided the book into three parts: (1) the divorce industry, (2) well families, and (3) toward a well family industry.

Booher, Dianna Daniels. **Coping . . . When Your Family Falls Apart.** New York: Messner, 1979. 192p.

This guide explores the emotional responses to divorce and offers older teenagers reassurance and recommendations for adjustment and acceptance.

Diamond, Susan Arnsberg. **Helping Children of Divorce: A Handbook for Parents and Teachers.** New York: Schocken, 1986. 130p.

The author suggests ways teachers and parents can expand on current practices to help children during and after the trauma of divorce. Examples of insensitive actions and remarks are given, along with positive alternatives.

Duncan, Lois. **Chapters: My Growth as a Writer.** Boston: Little, Brown, 1982. 263p.

In the story of her life, especially as seen through her writing for young adults, Lois Duncan tells about her divorce and the events that surrounded it.

Ferrara, Frank. **On Being Father: A Divorced Man Talks about Sharing the New Responsibility of Parenthood.** Garden City, NY: Doubleday, 1985. 175p.

This book offers advice to the newly divorced father about such issues as recreating the family, running the home as a single father, and dealing with an ex-wife.

Friedman, James T. **The Divorce Handbook: Your Basic Guide to Divorce.** New York: Random House, 1982. 170p.

Written for the lay audience by an authority in family law. The author translates legal jargon and the legal process from the beginning of the divorce to the end. Trends in family law in such areas as custody award and marital property laws are also discussed.

Gardner, Richard A. **The Parent's Book about Divorce.** New York: Doubleday, 1977. 368p.

A comprehensive guide for parents that includes a wealth of material on topics including guilt and shame, post-separation adjustment and problems, and children's involvement with professional counselors.

Gilbert, Sara. **Trouble at Home.** New York: Lothrop, Lee & Shephard, 1981. 191p.

A practical guide that examines positive responses to many issues of concern to children, including separation and divorce.

Goldstein, Sonja, and Albert J. Solnit. **Divorce and Your Child: Practical Suggestions for Parents.** New Haven, CT: Yale University Press, 1984. 160p.

The authors, a lawyer and a psychiatrist, discuss the problems for children in a family that is going through a divorce, both during the proceedings and after the divorce becomes final.

Goldzband, Melvin G. **Quality Time: Easing the Children through Divorce.** New York: McGraw-Hill, 1985.

Emphasizing the quality rather than the amount of the time the child spends with each parent, the author focuses on the children of divorce and what is best for them.

Hausslein, Evelyn B. **Children and Divorce: An Annotated Bibliography and Guide.** New York: Garland, 1983. 130p.

This bibliography brings together publications from many different disciplines and suggests professionals and laypeople for whom they may be useful. Books and articles written from 1975 to 1980 and available to the public make up the major part of the bibliography. One section consists of items appropriate for children and young adults, while another is a list of audiovisual materials on divorce.

Hyde, Margaret Oldroyd. **My Friend Has Four Parents.** New York: McGraw-Hill, 1981. 120p.

The author examines various situations that arise from divorce and remarriage. Information is included on custody and parental kidnapping.

Jackson, Michael, and Jessica Jackson. **Your Father's Not Coming Home Anymore.** New York: R. Marek, 1981. 320p.

A record of interviews with 30 teenagers, mostly of high school age, who tell how they coped with their parents' divorce.

Krementz, Jill. **How It Feels When Parents Divorce.** New York: Alfred A. Knopf, 1984. 115p.

In sensitive accounts, 19 young people give their impressions of their parents' divorce and how it affected their lives. Includes photographs.

Laiken, Deidre S. **Daughters of Divorce: The Effects of Parental Divorce on Women's Lives.** New York: Wm. Morrow, 1981. 201p.

Through interviews with analysts, psychiatrists, and women (ages 20–50), this book explores the impact of parental divorce on daughters' later relationships with men.

List, Julie. **The Day the Loving Stopped: A Daughter's View of Her Parents' Divorce.** New York: Seaview, 1980. 215p.

A deeply personal account of a child's experience of her parent's divorce. Her painful memories, recorded in letters to her father and in a journal, include her feelings about her parents' arguing and about exchanging a full-time father for a weekend father.

McGuire, Paula. **Putting It Together: Teenagers Talk about Family Breakup.** New York: Delacorte, 1987. 167p.

The author interviewed more than 20 children, teenagers, and professional counselors about the effects of family breakups. A strong sense of resilience emerges through the young people's accounts.

Meyers, Susan, and Joan Lakan. **Who Will Take the Children? A New Custody Option for Divorcing Mothers—and Fathers.** Indianapolis: Bobbs-Merrill, 1983. 211p.

A story written by two mothers whose children were in the custody of their fathers after the divorce.

Napolitane, Catherine, and Victoria Pellegrino. **Living and Loving after Divorce.** New York: Rawson Associates, 1977. 308p.

Part One offers advice about how to deal with various problems of divorce; Part Two identifies eight stages a divorced person goes through: The Active Bleeder, Euphoria, Running, All Work and No Play, Post-Love Blues, Yahoo!, Post-Yahoo, and The Search for the Real Me.

Richards, Arlene, and Irene Willis. **How To Get It Together When Your Parents Are Coming Apart.** New York: Bantam, 1976. 171p.

This book for adolescents deals with family troubles before, during, and after the divorce. Normally adolescents have more questions about relationships and decisions than do younger children, yet communicate less with their parents. The authors try to show that not all marital conflicts lead to divorce and that the process can be understood at all stages.

Robson, Bonnie. **My Parents Are Divorced Too.** New York: Everest House, 1980. 208p.

The author, a child psychiatrist, presents a summary of interviews with 28 young people, aged 12 to 17, whose parents have divorced.

Rofes, Eric E., and the students at Fayerweather Street School. **The Kids' Book of Divorce: By, for and about Kids.** Lexington, MA: Lewis Publishing, 1981. 123p.

Written by students of Fayerweather Street School in Cambridge, Massachusetts, who had experienced divorce and who felt the information available to kids was inadequate to prepare them for new relationships with their parents. Among the topics discussed are how to relate to counselors and the issue of living with gay parents.

Rowland, Peter. **Saturday Parent: A Book for Separated Families.** New York: Continuum, 1980. 143p.

The author interviewed many noncustodial parents who see their children "only on Saturday." He concludes that it is important and worthwhile for noncustodial parents to stay in touch with their children even though they no longer live together.

Salk, Lee. **What Every Child Would Like Parents To Know about Divorce.** New York: Harper & Row, 1978. 149p.

A guide for parents that includes such topics as the impact of divorce on children, what to tell children, questions of custody, and dealing with the legal system.

Sell, Kenneth D., compiler. **Divorce in the 70s: A Subject Bibliography.** Phoenix, AZ: Oryx, 1981. 191p.

A comprehensive compilation of a number of studies, articles, books, and nonprint materials on the topic of divorce, indexed by subject, author, and geographic area.

Smith, C. W. **Will They Love Me When I Leave? A Weekend Father's Struggle To Stay Close to His Kids.** New York: Putnam, 1987. 224p.

A sensitive and powerfully written memoir about the experience of being a divorced father.

Turow, Rita. **Daddy Doesn't Live Here Anymore.** Matteson, IL: Greatlakes Living Press, 1977. 196p.

The author discusses the emotional effects of divorce on children and suggests ways to help them adjust.

Walker, Glynnis. **Solomon's Children: Exploding the Myths of Divorce.** New York: Arbor House, 1986. 218p.

The author explodes some of the myths of divorce, basing her conclusions on questionnaire responses from 368 children of divorced parents. The average age of respondents at the time of the divorce was 11; the median age at the time of the survey was 19. Among the participants, Walker found an eagerness to express their opinions, struggles with guilt over the divorce, and a widely held feeling that fathers are indispensable and should be given the same right to custody that mothers have traditionally had.

Wallerstein, Judith S., and Joan Berlin Kelly. **Surviving the Breakup: How Children and Parents Cope with Divorce.** New York: Basic Books, 1980. 341p.

Based on 60 families who were followed for five years after divorce, the authors present a study that looks at the event's immediate and long-range effects on children . The study concentrated on determining what helps children ages 3–18 survive divorce and what inhibits their recovery. The researchers found that the children's relationships to their fathers did not diminish in importance despite infrequent contact, and that children's anger and yearnings endure over years.

Weitzman, Lenore J. **The Divorce Revolution: The Unexpected Social and Economic Consequences for Women and Children in America.** New York: Free Press, 1985. 401p.

Based on a ten-year study, the author presents the first hard facts about the consequences of the divorce revolution: divorced women and their children suffer an immediate 73 percent drop in their standard of living, while their ex-husbands enjoy a 42 percent rise in theirs. Weitzman analyzed court records and interviewed hundreds of judges, attorneys, and recently divorced men and women.

ARTICLES

Brophy, Beth. **"Children under Stress,"** *U.S. News & World Report* 101, no. 17 (27 October 1986): 58–63.

Divorce is one aspect of stress explored in this article. The authors cite divided opinions on the long-term effects of divorce on children.

Conant, Jennet. **"You'd Better Sit Down, Kids,"** *Newsweek* 110, no. 8 (24 August 1987): 58.

The authors believe the age and sex of the children, their relationship with their parents, and their memories of pre-divorce family life all contribute to children's adjustment or lack of adjustment after a divorce.

Glenn, Norval D. **"Children of Divorce,"** *Psychology Today* 19, no. 6 (June 1985): 68–69.

When adult children of divorce were compared with others on eight measures of psychological well-being, they were found to compare unfavorably on almost all of the measures. Although the author is tentative about the results, he suggests there is reason for concern.

Norton, Arthur J., and Jeanne E. Moorman. **"Current Trends in Marriage and Divorce among American Women,"** *Journal of Marriage and the Family* 49, no. 1 (February 1987): 3–14.

This study is based on data from the June 1985 Current Population Survey conducted by the Bureau of the Census. It examines recent trends and future prospects regarding marriage and divorce patterns among women in the United States.

Vaughan, Diane. **"The Long Goodbye,"** *Psychology Today* 21, no. 7 (July 1987): 37–42.

The author interviewed counselors, collected case histories, and sat in on group sessions for separated and divorced people. She found that secrecy and cover-up in failing relationships often hide problems until it is too late to solve them and that breakdowns in communication represent a basic problem.

Nonprint Materials on Divorce

Dear Mr. Henshaw

Type:	Filmstrips with audiocassettes or video
Length:	50 min., 34 min. (2 filmstrips); 31 min. (video)
Cost:	Purchase $55 (filmstrips), $69.95 (video)
Distributor:	McGraw-Hill Films
	Education Resources
	P.O. Box 408
	Hight's Town, NJ 08520
Date:	1985

A live-action filmstrip version of Beverly Cleary's Newbery Award book. Leigh Botts, aged 12, has problems. His parents are divorced and he is having difficulty adjusting to a new school. His loneliness is eased through the letters he writes to Mr. Henshaw, an author.

Divorce: A Teenage Perspective

Type:	16mm film or video
Length:	15 min.
Cost:	Purchase $250 (film); rental $40, purchase $225 (video)

Distributor: MTI Teleprograms Inc.
              108 Wilmot Road
              Deerfield, IL 60015-9990
Date: 1986

Three adolescents who feel their families are the only ones having problems discuss how they are coping with their parents' divorces.

The Divorce Express

Type: 3 filmstrips with 3 audiocassettes
Length: 12–15 min.
Cost: Purchase $79.95
Distributor: Cheshire Corp.
              514 Bryant Street
              Palo Alto, CA 94301
Date: 1984

Based on Paula Danziger's book, this presentation delves into the life of ninth grader Phoebe Brooks, whose parents are divorced. Phoebe must commute between her father's home in Woodstock and her mother's in New York City.

Divorce from Family Life: Transitions in Marriage

Type: 16mm color film
Length: 16 min.
Cost: Rental $13
Distributor: Centron Films
              108 Wilmot Road
              Deerfield, IL 60015-9990
Date: 1981

When Helene and Alan reach the crisis point in their marriage and announce their intention to separate, their children's reactions range from fear to guilt to anger. As the children struggle to adjust to the new realities of their family life, the parents must deal with the divorce issue. From the series A Case History.

Divorce Wars

Type: All video formats
Length: 58 min.
Cost: Rental $95, purchase $300
Distributor: PBS Video
              1320 Braddock Place
              Alexandria, VA 22314-1698
Date: 1986

Centering solely on Delaware, this intriguing "Frontline" documentary examines divorce and its impact on the family.

Jen

Type:	1/2" VHS video
Length:	27 min.
Cost:	Rental $12
Distributor:	Beacon Films
	930 Pitner Avenue
	Evaston, IL 60202
Date:	1983

Teenage Jen returns from summer camp to discover that her parents have separated and agreed on a split custody arrangement for her. Her initial feelings of guilt, confusion, and pain evolve into resentment that she was not included in the decision. From the series Coming of Age.

Me and Dad's New Wife

Type:	16mm film
Length:	33 min.
Cost:	Rental $16
Distributor:	Time-Life Video
	Time & Life Building
	1271 Avenue of the Americas
	New York, NY 10020
Date:	1976

Based on Stella Pevsner's book *A Smart Kid Like You*, this is the story of 12-year-old Nina, who has been treated maturely and with consideration by her divorced parents, and who discovers on her first day in junior high school that her new math teacher is her father's new wife. From the series The Teenage Years.

Memories of Family

Type:	16mm film
Length:	24 min.
Cost:	Rental $45, purchase $425
Distributor:	Polymorph Films
	118 South Street
	Boston, MA 02111
Date:	1977

In six scenes, family members recall other family members who are gone as the result of divorce.

Mothers after Divorce

Type:	16mm film
Length:	20 min.
Cost:	Rental $12.50

Distributor: Polymorph Films
118 South Street
Boston, MA 02111
Date: 1976

Four women with children of high school age—women who led protected lives until divorce—talk openly about their new lives, including sharing responsibilities with children and helping children trust and love.

Separation/Divorce: It Has Nothing To Do with You

Type: 16mm film
Length: 14 min.
Cost: Rental $9
Distributor: McGraw-Hill Films
Education Resources
P.O. Box 408
Hight's Town, NJ 08520
Date: 1974

Larry's parents have decided to separate and he finds he will have to choose between them. From the series Conflict and Awareness.

Table for One

Type: 16mm film or video
Length: 28 min.
Cost: Rental $150, purchase $575 (film); purchase $275 (video)
Distributor: Doris Chase Concepts
222 W. 23rd
New York, NY 10011
Date: 1985

A dramatic monologue uses voice-over techniques and flashbacks to illustrate a woman dining alone in a restaurant and thinking about her life and why she left her husband.

The Way It Is: After the Divorce

Type: 16mm film or video
Length: 24 min.
Cost: Purchase $440 (film); rental $40, purchase $350 (video)
Distributor: National Film Board of Canada
1251 Avenue of the Americas, 16th Floor
New York, NY 10020
Date: 1983

A woman and her daughter cope with the aftermath of divorce, unrealistic hopes, and increased responsibilities.

When Divorce Comes to School

Type:	Video
Length:	28 min.
Cost:	Rental $40, purchase $295
Distributor:	Education Development Center
	Distribution Center
	39 Chapel Street
	Newton, MA 02160
Date:	1984

One school's approach to helping students cope with their parents' divorce.

Organizations Concerned with Divorce

Adam and Eve
1008 White Oak
Arlington Heights, IL 60005
(312) 870-1040
Executive Director: Louis J. Filczer

Provides divorce counseling and mediation as well as information on divorce reform and implementation of new divorce procedures. Conducts research programs, conferences, and seminars.

PUBLICATION: Newsletter (periodic).

Committee for Mother and Child Rights
Route 1, Box 256A
Clearbrook, VA 22624
(703) 722-3652
Codirector: Elizabeth Owen

A national organization offering emotional support for mothers with custody problems and attempting to correct the injustices to mothers and children that often occur with divorce. The group is advisory and provides a network and referrals.

Divorce Reform
P.O. Box 243
Kenwood, CA 95452
(707) 833-2550
President: George Partis

This group is especially interested in establishing Family Arbitration Centers in lieu of divorce courts and gives advice in setting up such centers. Members advocate getting divorce out of the courts and the establishment of a Department of Family Relations under the executive branch of every state government.

PUBLICATION: *Divorce Chats* (periodic).

National Council for Children's Rights
2001 O Street NW
Washington, DC 20036
(202) 223-6227
President: David L. Levy

Favoring joint custody, mediation, visitation enforcement, and equitable child support, this group conducts research, monitors legislation, and sponsors educational seminars. Audiocassettes, model bills, legal briefs, and other materials are available from the council.

PUBLICATION: *Speak Out for Children* newsletter (quarterly).

Parents Sharing Custody
435 N. Bedford Drive, Suite 310
Beverly Hills, CA 90210
(213) 476-7862
President: Linda Blakeley

An organization concerned with parents sharing custody of children after divorce and protecting the right of children to have access to both parents. Helps with referrals for counseling and networks across the country.

Parents Without Partners
8807 Colesville Road
Silver Spring, MD 20910
(301) 588-9354
President: Richard Stewart

A comprehensive, international, nonsectarian organization that is concerned with the welfare of single parents and their children. It includes over 600 chapters throughout the United States and in some foreign countries. A new affiliate is The International Youth Council for young people ages 12 to 17.

PUBLICATIONS: *Single Parents*, *International Youth* newsletter.

CHAPTER 9

Child Abuse

When Georgie regained consciousness the dimly lighted apartment seemed to be full of people. The first person he saw was a young woman in a nurse's uniform who leaned over him as he lay on the sofa, bathing his head and neck, laying soft bandages across his wounds. He gave a choking gasp as he realized where he was and tried to get up, looking wildly about the apartment to see if Steve lurked somewhere in the shadows.

Irene Hunt, *The Lottery Rose* (New York: Scribner's, 1976), 33.

Seven-and-one-half-year-old Georgie is beaten so often by Steve, his mother's boyfriend, that he is always wary of him. He has learned where to hide and what to do and say so as to call the least amount of attention to himself. In the scene above, Georgie is almost killed by Steve. Georgie's mother and Steve should be taken to court for the way they treat him, but Georgie is afraid that if that happens he will have no place to go and no one to help him. He fears more beatings if he reports his home life to the authorities, and he believes that his miserable home is better than no home at all. So he lies to teachers when they ask him about his bruises and cuts. When he is finally taken to a Catholic boys' home, it is a long time before he trusts any of the adults there.

The broom crashed down on her shoulder with numbing force, and she heard Tim cry out in protest, and then another blow landed against the side of her head so that there was a ringing sound in her ears.

"Stop it!" Tim was yelling. "Stop it, I'll tell my dad on you! Don't hurt Laurie!" Laurie kept backing toward the door, feeling as if she were in the midst of some terrible

nightmare. But she didn't awaken, and the blows rained
down on her head and shoulders. . . .

> Willo Davis Roberts, *Don't Hurt Laurie!* (New York:
> Atheneum, 1977), 135.

Abby was beautiful, that was for sure, and there were many
times I [Chip, her high school boyfriend] wanted to hold
her . . . but I was me, not her father; and what about Pete
[Abby's little sister]? All those Saturday mornings when
Abby got Pete out of the house for swimming or took her to
the park. . . . Things like this just didn't happen. Oh, maybe
in really poor families or with alcoholics or drug pushers,
but not with families who lived just down the street, not to
girls like Abby. If it was true, how could Mrs. Morris not
know it, and if she knew it, how could she let it happen?

> Hadley Irwin, *Abby, My Love* (New York:
> Atheneum, 1985), 117.

Although these examples are from works of fiction, such circumstances are not unusual in real life. The abuser in each of these cases
was someone in the family who should have been protecting the
young person, someone the young person was supposed to be able
trust. Because this important relationship was destroyed, the young
person felt no one could be trusted. In two of the stories, *The Lottery
Rose* and *Don't Hurt Laurie!*, someone at school had thought about
reporting the abuse. In Laurie's story she objected, claiming she had
had an accident, while in *The Lottery Rose*, Georgie maintained he
had been in a fight with peers.

Child abuse has been defined as "physical or mental injury, sexual
abuse, negligent treatment or maltreatment of a child under the age of
18 by a person who is responsible for the child's health or welfare
under circumstances which indicate that the child's welfare is
harmed or threatened" (O'Brien, 1980, 9).

Statistics about Child Abuse

Statistics reveal the frightening enormity of the problem in our society:

- Estimates indicate that at least 2 and as many as 15 children
  die each day from abuse (ibid., 35).

- Some estimates indicate that, on the average, abuse claims a child's life every four hours (ibid.).
- In 1985, there were 1,299,400 reported cases of child abuse in the United States, twice as many as were reported in 1978 (*Statistical Abstract, 1988,* 164).
- The average age of children involved in abuse was 7; 21 percent were over the age of 12 (Flanigan, 3).
- Fifty-two percent of the abused children reported were female (ibid.).
- Studies show that as many as 80 percent of prison inmates and prostitutes were abused as children (Heger, 66).

Physical Abuse

Physical abuse involves behavior that results in bodily injury from hitting, kicking, or rough handling. It is also considered abuse if a child is inadequately supervised by a parent or guardian, or if a physical injury results from hazardous conditions uncorrected by a parent or guardian.

Adults who work with children, such as teachers, are required to report cases of suspected or known physical abuse. Children who are physically abused sometimes bear signs of injury such as bruises, welts, burns, fractures, swellings, or lost teeth. Older children may attribute the injury to some accident, fearing retaliation by a parent. Abused children may be habitually truant or late to school. Sometimes a parent keeps the injured child at home until the evidence of abuse disappears. Abused children may often be tired and sleep in class. They may be inappropriately dressed for the weather, wearing clothing with long sleeves or high necklines on hot days to hide bruises or burns, or wearing insufficient clothing to be comfortable on cold days (Hennepin, 19).

Sexual Abuse

Sexual abuse is the use of a child by an adult for his or her sexual gratification without consideration of the child's psyche or development. Children and adolescents need to be aware of the possibility of such treatment from family members and friends, as well as from strangers. Sexual abuse by a relative is called incest and is much more common than abuse by strangers. Books are now available to explain to children the difference between touches that make them feel good and touches that make them feel bad. The books teach that touches should never be secret (Hittleman, 34).

According to the 1984 Congressional Committee Report on Children, Youth, and Families, our knowledge of sexual abuse in the 1980s is about where our knowledge of physical child abuse was in the 1950s. "We are scared to admit the fact that it [sexual abuse] is probably at the same level [as physical abuse]" (U.S. House of Representatives, 169).

- From 1983 to 1984, reports of sexual abuse of children increased 59 percent ("Child Sex Abuse Said To Rise").
- Most of the children are abused at home by parents (ibid.).
- In 1985 a national poll of 2,627 randomly selected adults found that 22 percent had been victims of sexual abuse (Heger, 66).
- Only one in every five or six sexual abuse victims is abused by a total stranger; the other cases of sexual abuse involve a family member or relative (Leo, 72).
- Of 930 women surveyed in San Francisco (reported in 1984), 38 percent said they had been abused by the age of 18 and 28 percent by the age of 14 (ibid.).
- In 1984, 958,590 child abuse and neglect cases were reported, which was up 16 percent since 1983, representing the largest one-year increase ever recorded ("Child Sex Abuse Said To Rise"). Although the number of reported abuse cases is rising, many experts believe that a great many cases go unreported because typically the abuser is in a position of trust with the child.

Psychological Abuse

Psychological abuse is the destruction of the self-confidence and self-esteem of a child until the child thinks he or she can do nothing correctly. Constant belittling, ignoring, and rejecting are damaging to the person who is the target of such behavior.

Dr. James Garbarino, author with Edna Guttman and Janis Wilson Seeley of *The Psychologically Battered Child*, believes psychological maltreatment of a child leaves scars that can last a lifetime. An occasional incident does not cause lasting harm, but chronic patterns are harmful. Garbarino puts psychological abuse into five categories:

1. Rejecting. The child feels rejected because he or she apparently can do nothing to please the parent. The adult refuses to acknowledge the child's worth and the legitimacy of the child's needs (Garbarino et al., 8).
2. Isolating. The adult cuts the child off from normal social experiences, prevents the child from forming friendships,

and makes the child believe that he or she is alone in the world (ibid.).

3. Terrorizing. The adult verbally assaults the child, creates a climate of fear, bullies and frightens the child, and makes the child believe that the world is capricious and hostile (ibid.).

4. Ignoring. The adult deprives the child of essential stimulation and responsiveness, stifling emotional growth and intellectual development (ibid.).

5. Corrupting. The adult "mis-socializes" the child, stimulates the child to engage in destructive antisocial behavior, reinforces that deviance, and makes the child unfit for normal social experiences (ibid.).

Neglect

Neglect encompasses both psychological and physical abuse. Neglected children are those who "must search for food when they are hungry and often go without; they fall asleep wherever they are when exhausted; they appear to wander aimlessly in homes that are disorganized, 'without warmth and without meaning'" (Brenner, 50). Neglect of practically any type that impairs a child's development constitutes abuse.

Sometimes a parent is absorbed in other problems and is not aware of the effect this neglect is having on the child. "Some neglected children are physically well cared for, but have parents who give no love or attention, no moral guidance, no praise or punishment. According to the National Center on Child Abuse and Neglect, these emotionally neglectful parents encourage antisocial behavior, including drug and alcohol abuse, by refusing to know or care what happens to their children" (ibid.).

As with cases of child abuse in general, statistics on child neglect are hard to obtain since the number of cases that actually occur and the number reported may differ greatly. National figures indicate neglect cases constituted 45.7 percent of reported abuse while deprivation of necessities constituted 58.4 percent of reported abuse (Flanigan, 3).

Who Are the Abusers?

To the average American, child abuse conjures up the picture of a sadist who batters or deliberately neglects innocent children to fulfill a ghoulish set of psychological perversions. Many people who abuse their children do not fit into the category of deliberate perpetrators. Instead, they are troubled, isolated individuals, often as much victims as the children they abuse. Slightly less than ten percent of abusive parents have severe psychological problems. These groups appear to have a higher potential as abusers:

1. Persons who are unemployed. There appears to be a pattern connecting increased family violence with increased unemployment. Child abuse fluctuated in concert with unemployment, peaking in 1974 and 1982, and declining for the years in between. In 1982, in two Wisconsin counties, a three percent increase in unemployment was paralleled by a 125 percent increase in reports of abuse and neglect (U.S. House of Representatives, 58).

2. Persons who were themselves abused as children. One report indicated that as many as 85 percent of all parents who abuse their children were abused themselves (O'Brien, 1984, 35).

3. Persons becoming parents at younger ages are at greater risk of being involved in child abuse (Flanigan, 3). Many of these families are living on a low income, which adds to their stress.

Child abusers appear to be present in all social groups and classes of our society. The average age of offenders is 31, and 60 percent of offenders are female (ibid.). Abusers are often under stress, either internally or externally.

In addition to the unemployed, those in lower income levels have a disproportionately large number of abuse cases. Poorer families experience more stress, since they are less able to have time away from their children, hire babysitters or send their children to camp, allowing for less separation between the parents and children who may have behavior problems. In addition, single parents are more often living in poverty income levels, making them a higher risk for child abuse (Zigler and Rubin, 106).

Abusive families are often in social isolation, removed from family support systems, with unlisted telephone numbers and few friends (ibid., 215). Parents who are not informed about child development and childrearing practices often show less tolerance for the child's viewpoint. Zigler also feels Americans glorify violence, which is reflected in the acceptance of using physical means to control children (ibid., 216).

Social scientists today are moving toward an understanding of abuse called "interactive." Many social scientists believe that abuse is the result of a combination of personal and external social factors. They point out that the more stresses a parent operates under, the more likely he or she is to abuse a child.

Who Are the Abused?

All children are susceptible to abuse. Parents sometimes get impatient with babies' crying, but teenagers are also vulnerable to abuse, especially from parents who do not adapt well to their physical changes and increasing signs of maturity. Certain types of children have been observed to be at high risk for abuse. For example, children and teenagers with "difficult temperaments" are sometimes targets for abuse. These may be bright kids who want to know reasons for parental demands and whose questions appear impertinent to an impatient parent.

Abused children may develop behavior patterns that make them targets for more abuse. For example, a mother may discover that hitting a disobedient child changes his behavior temporarily. If the child continues to disobey, the mother may persist in physical punishment, and the abuse escalates. Children who are abused may lag developmentally, and this very characteristic may provoke an abusive parent further. Some abused kids are timid and can not live up to the image demanded by an aggressive parent. Hostility, aggression, and poor self-esteem are other characteristics that abused children may have.

A fine line exists between legitimate punishment and child abuse. Parents who believe they will "spoil the child" if they "spare the rod" may be doing what they think is right and what would have been applauded 100 years ago. However, over the last ten years, spanking of children has come to be regarded differently. Welsh believes spanking is part of "severe parental punishment" and that it is the most significant precursor to delinquency. In Welsh's study of fantasy aggression, his results suggest that both fear and anger occur in a child when spanked, but rarely is the child's anger acted out toward the parent. In most instances, it becomes inappropriately displaced toward society. The more violent the childrearing practices in a culture, the greater the probability that the culture will be crime-ridden (Welsh, 27).

Reporting Abuse

Children who are being abused are usually too fearful of the consequences to report the abuse to authorities themselves. Even though their situation may be intolerable, they may believe it could be worse if they reported it. Visions of being removed from their home to some unknown place or of parents being put in jail can be immobilizing to children. They don't know whom they can trust and are too uncertain of the outcome.

Professionals, such as educators, dentists, doctors, law enforcement officers, nurses, and foster parents, are mandated by law to report cases of neglect, physical abuse, and sexual abuse that have affected children or that are currently endangering them. Any private citizen can report child abuse, sexual abuse, or neglect as well. Some areas have a hotline that allows individuals to call 24 hours a day for help.

Social service agencies also accept child abuse reports from individuals. The kinds of information that will be required from persons reporting suspected or known instances of abuse include:

1. The identity of the child
2. What happened to the child
3. When the abuse occurred
4. The source of the information provided
5. The child's present location
6. The names and addresses of the parents
7. The name and telephone number of the person filing the report

If a child is believed to be in imminent danger, the local police department or sheriff's office should be called immediately. Officers can remove a minor (a child under 18 years of age) from a threatening environment in order to protect him or her.

The police or agency contacted has an obligation to respond promptly to any reports of child abuse or neglect. They need to determine what the risks are for further injury and gather facts about the persons involved. They will plan a course of treatment, deciding if the family remains together during treatment or if they need to be separated. When possible, the offending parent will be removed from the home. Sometimes the child will stay with a relative, maintaining the family identity and making it easier for the family to get back together again.

There is considerable evidence that child abuse continues to occur in our society even though the law, the medical profession, social service agencies, and others are working hard to identify abusers and protect the abused. There is concern for the cycle of abuse, which demonstrates that those who were abused as children often become child abusers as adults. All segments of our society need to work together to break this cycle.

Each state has a system for finding the abusers and the abused. Bringing the abusers to justice, getting treatment for them, and helping the abused to establish a secure life-style are all important. Each person has a responsibility to help make the laws work and to protect the rights of children.

REFERENCES

Brenner, Avis. "Wednesday's Child," *Psychology Today* 19, no. 5 (May 1985): 46–50.

"Child Sex Abuse Said To Rise," *New York Times*, 19 March 1986.

Flanigan, Barbara, editor. *Protecting Minnesota's Children: Public Issues*. St. Paul: League of Women Voters of Minnesota, 1986.

Garbarino, James, Edna Guttman, and Janis Wilson Seeley. *The Psychologically Battered Child*. San Francisco: Jossey-Bass, 1986.

Heger, Astrid. "Helping Molested Children," *U.S. News & World Report* 100, no. 9 (10 March 1986): 66.

Hennepin County Child Protection and Public Affairs. *Child Abuse and Neglect: Hennepin County Guide for People Who Work with Children*. Minneapolis, MN: 1984.

Hittleman, Margo. "Sexual Abuse: Teaching about Touching," *School Library Journal* 31, no. 5 (January 1985): 34–35.

Hunt, Irene. *The Lottery Rose*. New York: Scribner's, 1976.

Irwin, Hadley. *Abby, My Love*. New York: Atheneum, 1985.

Leo, John. "Some Day I'll Cry My Eyes Out," *Time* 123, no. 17 (23 April 1984): 72–73.

O'Brien, Shirley. *Child Abuse: A Crying Shame*. Provo, UT: Brigham Young University Press, 1980.

——. "Child Abuse and Neglect: Everyone's Problem," ERIC Documents, Report No. ED 250 845, ISBN-0-87173-106-1, 1984.

Roberts, Willo Davis. *Don't Hurt Laurie!* New York: Atheneum, 1977.

Statistical Abstract of the United States, 1986: National Data Book and Guide to Sources, 106th edition. Washington, DC: Government Printing Office, 1986.

U.S. House of Representatives. *Children, Youth, and Families: 1983, A Year-End Report on the Activities of the Select Committee on Children, Youth and Families*. Washington, DC: Government Printing Office, 1984.

Welsh, Ralph S. "Spanking: A Grand Old American Tradition?" *Children Today* 14, no. 1 (January/February 1985): 25–29.

Zigler, Edward, and Nancy Rubin. "Why Child Abuse Occurs," *Parents* 60, no. 11 (November 1985): 102–106, 215–218.

Resources
for Finding Out about Child Abuse

Fiction about Child Abuse

Armstrong, Louise. **Saving the Big-Deal Baby.** Black and white illustrations by Jack Hearne. New York: Dutton "Skinny Book," 1980. 42p.

Teenage mother Janine has fallen into a pattern of taking out her frustrations on her 14-month-old son, P.J. Her 19-year-old husband, Robbie, reacts with violence toward her because of her behavior with the baby. A parents' help-group provides the young couple with insights into their problems and support for their frustrations.

Ashely, Bernard. **Break in the Sun.** Black and white illustrations by Charles Keeping. New York: S. G. Phillips, 1980. 185p.

Eleven-year-old Patsy Bligh runs away to escape an abusive stepfather. By the time he finds her, both have gained some insight into themselves and each other. Set in England.

Bauer, Marion Dane. **Foster Child.** Somers, CT: Seabury Press (Dell Paperback), 1977. 155p.

A series of shocks—the sudden illness and imminent death of a substitute parent, sexual advances by a frightening man, a realization of danger to herself and a friend—force 12-year-old Renny to make some adult decisions.

Borich, Michael. **A Different Kind of Love.** New York: Holt, Rinehart & Winston, 1985. 165p.

Lonely, 14-year-old Elizabeth is caught between real love for her handsome young visiting uncle (a rock musician) and confusion over his physical overtures, which she experiences as pleasant at first and then threatening.

Bulla, Clyde Robert. **Almost a Hero.** Black and white illustrations by Ben Stahl. New York: Dutton "Skinny Book," 1981. 40p.

A young man narrates his return to the orphanage where he was abused and to the woman who swindled him out of his earnings. He finds his planned revenge meaningless.

Byars, Betsy. **Cracker Jackson.** New York: Viking Kestrel, 1985. 146p.

Eleven-year-old Cracker is instrumental in getting his ex-babysitter Alma to seek shelter from her husband, Billy Ray, who beats her and their baby. Billy Ray's anger is also directed at Cracker and his friends for meddling.

Cullin, Charlotte. **Cages of Glass, Flowers of Time.** New York: Bradbury (Dell Paperback), 1979. 316p.

Claire, now 14, tells her story as an abused, brutalized young girl struggling to escape her terrifying life but reluctant to trust anyone who tries to help her. Claire's pathetic mother learned abuse from her own brutal mother. Fortunately, Claire discovers she has artistic talents and finds help to develop these and also to deal with her mother.

Dahl, Roald. **Boy: Tales of Childhood.** New York: Farrar, Straus & Giroux, 1984. 160p.

Although his home life was happy, the writer recollects with vivid horror the constant beatings and canings that were common at English boarding schools earlier in the century.

Greene, Bette. **The Summer of My German Soldier.** New York: Dial, 1973. 230p.

Twelve-year-old Patty Bergen is continually ridiculed and occasionally beaten by her father, causing her to look for support from a compassionate black housekeeper and for love from an escaped German prisoner of war.

Hall, Lynn. **The Boy in the Off-White Hat.** New York: Scribner, 1984. 87p.

A 13-year-old mother's helper discovers that her young charge, Shane, is being sexually abused by a man supposedly courting his mother.

Hamilton, Virginia. **Sweet Whispers, Brother Rush.** New York: Avon, 1982. 215p.

Tree, a young black girl, and her ill brother are visited by a ghost who helps Tree understand their mother's background of abuse and why she must leave them alone for days while she works as a practical nurse.

Hermes, Patricia. **A Solitary Secret.** New York: Harcourt Brace Jovanovich, 1985. 135p.

A 14-year-old girl tells the story of how her mother took her 6-year-old brother and just quietly disappeared. She is left as the housekeeper for her father, a lumberyard worker, who begins molesting her sexually. She is fearful of his threats, but tells her story in her journal and eventually to the mother of a friend. Poignant and understated.

Howard, Ellen. **Gillyflower.** New York: Atheneum, 1986. 198p.

Sexually abused by her father and fearing for the safety of her younger sister, Gilly seeks the courage to tell someone what is happening.

Hunt, Irene. **The Lottery Rose.** New York: Scribner's (Tempo: Berkley Publishing paperback), 1976. 185p.

Seven-and-one-half-year-old Georgie, who is abused physically and emotionally by his mother and her boyfriend, wins a rosebush in a lottery and eventually learns to trust people in his new surroundings.

Irwin, Hadley. **Abby, My Love.** New York: Macmillan, 1985. 168p.

In this story told through the eyes of her high school boyfriend, Chip, the reader gradually realizes Abby is being sexually abused by her father. She finally tells Chip, who helps her and her family get help.

Levinson, Nancy Smiler. **Silent Fear.** Black and white illustrations by Paul Furan. Mankato, MN: Crestwood House, 1981. 63p.

In this high-interest and easy reading book, 13-year-old Sara's story focuses on her experiences in a new foster home where the mother beats her and threatens her and the other children if they say anything. Sara breaks the cycle of abuse, suggesting through the book that no situation is completely hopeless.

Magorian, Michelle. **Good Night, Mr. Tom.** New York: Harper & Row, 1981. 318p.

In this story set in World War II England, eight-year-old William is evacuated from London to live in a small town with Tom, a crusty widower in his sixties. William has been badly abused, wets his bed, and has never been in school. Tom and William have mutual needs for love.

Mazer, Harry. **The War on Villa Street: A Novel.** New York: Delacorte (Dell Paperback), 1978. 182p.

Willis Pierce, an eighth grader who is an outsider, has a drunken and abusive father. Willis acquires self-confidence through his success in track and his tutoring of a retarded boy. After his father beats him, Willis hits him back and then runs away from home. He returns home but vows not to be fearful of his father anymore.

Moeri, Louise. **The Girl Who Lived on the Ferris Wheel.** New York: Dutton (Avon paperback), 1979. 117p.

In 1943 in San Francisco, 11-year-old Til lives with her deranged mother who beats her and threatens to kill her with a butcher knife. Although Til sees her father on weekends, she is afraid to tell him or school officials of her fears. She eventually takes independent action and saves herself.

Newton, Suzanne. **I Will Call It Georgie's Blues.** New York: Viking, 1983. 197p.

Neal Sloan, the ninth-grade narrator, details the breakdown of his family, especially of his seven-year-old brother, Georgie, who becomes catatonic from the constant fear of his father, a rigid minister who psychologically abuses the children.

Reeves, Bruce. **Street Smarts.** New York: Beaufort Books, 1981. 222p.

Twelve-year-old T.C. lives in a commune in Berkeley, but she doesn't enjoy the environment there. She meets a boy from the area, eight-year-old Caper, who has never talked and who is physically abused by his mother and stepfather. After T.C. talks Caper into running away with her, they become street people and meet a strange assortment of characters.

Roberts, Willo Davis. **Don't Hurt Laurie!** New York: Atheneum, 1978. 166p.

Eleven-year-old Laurie is abused by her mother Annabelle, but is afraid to tell anyone, including her stepfather Jack, his two children Tim and Shelly, or his mother Nell. When Annabelle beats Laurie with a poker until she is unconscious, the children finally get help. Annabelle is hospitalized for mental illness and confesses she was an abused child herself and kept it a secret.

Strang, Celia. **Foster Mary.** New York: McGraw-Hill, 1979. 162p.

In the fall of 1959, 15-year-old Bud, the narrator, is one of several children who live with Mary and Alonzo in Yakima, Washington, where they have come to pick apples. Lonnie, who also lives with them, is a battered child with deep hostility. The life of migrant workers is portrayed.

Swartley, David Warren. **My Friend, My Brother.** Black and white illustrations by James Converse. Scottdale, PA: Herald Press, 1980. 102p.

Eric, a 12-year-old Mennonite, is taunted by Jon, a boy his age who is abused by his uncle and aunt. Jon's family falls apart and Eric's family adopts him when he becomes a ward of the court.

Whelan, Gloria. **A Time To Keep Silent.** New Jersey: Putnam, 1979. 127p.

Thirteen-year-old Claire stopped talking when her mother died and her father decided to start a mission in the wilderness. Claire meets Dorrie, a girl abused by her drunken father. Claire's first-person narration gives the reader insight into her grief, her concern for Dorrie, and Claire's own recovery.

Nonfiction Materials on Child Abuse

BOOKS AND PAMPHLETS

Broadhurst, Diane D. **The Educator's Role in the Prevention and Treatment of Child Abuse and Neglect.** Washington, DC: U.S. Department of Health, Education, and Welfare, 1979. 18p.

Contains sections on understanding child abuse and neglect and why educators should be involved; recognizing child abuse and neglect in the classroom setting; reporting child abuse and neglect; and after reporting a case, what schools can offer to those involved and how child abuse can be prevented.

Burch, Jennings Michael. **They Cage the Animals at Night.** New York: Signet, 1984. 293p.

A true story told as a flashback about the author's being abandoned in a Catholic children's home as an eight-year-old and being taken home by his mother several times, only to return to that home or others. The account of his miserable treatment and adults' cruelty and occasional kindness are written with pathos.

Child Abuse and Neglect Audiovisual Materials. Washington, DC: Government Printing Office, 1980.

This pamphlet contains an annotated list of audiovisual materials on child abuse and neglect, producer index, subject index, and title index.

Colao, Flora, and Tamar Hosansky. **Your Children Should Know: Teach Your Children the Strategies That Will Keep Them Safe from Assault and Crime.** Indianapolis: Bobbs-Merrill, 1983. 160p.

The authors present both physical self-defense skills and an assertiveness training program for children to enable them to stop the manipulating or bullying behavior of others.

Finkelhor, David. **Child Sexual Abuse: New Theory and Research.** New York: The Free Press, 1984. 260p.

The first four chapters are clearly written and describe the scope of this problem; research and current trends are explored.

————. **Sexually Victimized Children.** New York: The Free Press, 1979. 228p.

The description of the kind of people involved in child victimization is especially interesting. A personal account by an incest victim makes the facts come to life.

Garbarino, James, et al. **Protecting Children from Abuse and Neglect: Developing and Maintaining Effective Support Systems for Families.** San Francisco: Jossey-Bass, 1980. 222p.

Recognizing the personal networks of families and the role neighbors can play in helping with family problems, this book emphasizes the role of the social environment.

Garbarino, James, Edna Guttman, and Janis Wilson Seeley. **The Psychologically Battered Child.** San Francisco: Jossey-Bass, 1986. 286p.

A careful look at the causes of child psychological abuse and the behavior and symptoms of the psychologically abused child. The authors use case studies to illustrate their points.

Garbarino, James, and Gwen Gilliam. **Understanding Abusive Families.** Lexington, MA: Lexington Books, 1980. 263p.

The authors attempt to determine the causes of abuse in families, what relationships exist, and what action could curb these crimes.

Helfer, Ray E., and C. Henry Kempe. **Child Abuse and Neglect: The Family and the Community.** 3d edition. Cambridge, MA: Ballinger, 1980. 438p.

In this comprehensive book that focuses on child abuse and neglect, the authors look at child abuse development from early life through prevention and therapy.

Herbruck, Christine Comstock. **Breaking the Cycle of Child Abuse.** Minneapolis: Winston Press, 1979. 205p.

The focus is on the cycle of abuse: parents who are child abusers and who were abused children themselves. The parents have joined together to break the cycle. A Parents Anonymous group in Cleveland is used to show the education of parents in need of support and new coping skills.

Huchton, Laura M. **Protect Your Child: A Parent's Safeguard against Child Abduction and Sexual Abuse.** Englewood Cliffs, NJ: Prentice-Hall, 1985. 160p.

Emphasizing practical prevention measures, the author has included simple tests to stress safety awareness for children. Situations that are obviously threatening are presented with alternative ways of dealing with them. A written/oral safety test, which young people and their parents will find helpful, is included.

Kempe, C. Henry, and Ray E. Helfer. **The Battered Child.** 3d edition. Chicago: University of Chicago Press, 1980. 440p.

This book starts with a historical overview and a look at other cultures. Special problems such as alcohol and drug abuse are dealt with in the context of child abuse. The chapter on the consequences of abuse and neglect is particularly good.

Kempe, Ruth S., and C. Henry Kempe. **Child Abuse.** Cambridge, MA: Harvard University Press, 1978. 136p.

The section on the nature of child abuse is especially recommended. The book is also a good reference source for prevention and treatment questions.

————. **The Common Secret: Sexual Abuse of Children and Adolescents.** New York: W. H. Freeman, 1984. 284p.

Both authors have been involved in the field of child abuse studies for over 25 years. The nature of sexual abuse; its legal aspects; and evaluation, treatment, and prevention are presented in nontechnical terms.

Kraizer, Sherryll Kerns. **The Safe Child Book: A Commonsense Approach to Protecting Your Children from Abduction and Sexual Abuse.** Illustrated by Mary Kornblum. New York: Delacorte, 1985. 127p.

The purpose of this book is to give parents a basic understanding of sexual abuse and abduction and to provide specific personal safety training skills, techniques, and examples they can use with their children. Nevertheless, it also aims to help parents portray the world as a basically positive place for their children.

Landau, Hortense R., Marsha K. Salus, and Thelma Stiffarm. With Nora Lee Kalb. **Child Protection: The Role of the Courts.** Washington, DC: U.S. Department of Health and Human Services, 1980.

Beginning with an overview of child abuse and neglect, this pamphlet discusses how the court system relates to abuse victims and describes the process in juvenile court, case preparation, proving child maltreatment, use of witnesses, and court-ordered treatment. Includes a special section on court proceedings involving Indian children.

Lauderdale, Michael L., Rosalie N. Anderson, and Stephen E. Cramer, editors. **Child Abuse and Neglect: Issues on Innovation and Implementation, Vol. I.** Washington, DC: National Conference on Child Abuse and Neglect, 1977. DHEW Publication No. 78-30147.

Presented as conference papers, this edited volume makes the point that child abuse and neglect is not merely a private affair between caretaker and child, but rather a crisis that affects the entire community. A comprehensive overview of the issues.

Lynch, Margaret A., and Jacqueline Roberts. **Consequences of Child Abuse.** London: Academic Press, 1982. 226p.

For this folllow-up study of physically abused children, 41 out of the original sample of 42 children selected were located. Only 9 children were problem-free. The authors conclude that prevention is the only answer, not more and better treatment. The book includes helpful information for everyone.

Martin, Harold P. **Treatment for Abused and Neglected Children.** Washington, DC: U.S. Department of Health, Education, and Welfare, 1979. 9p.

Brief discussion of the need for treatment of abused and neglected children, including treatment of medical conditions related to neglect such as anemia, poor dental health, and vision problems and recommended treatment of developmental and psychological problems. The pamphlet also discusses changing the home environment to provide a safe place to live.

Mrazek, Patricia Beezley, and C. Henry Kempe, editors. **Sexually Abused Children and Their Families.** New York: Pergamon, 1981. 271p.

This book defines and gives a brief history of sexual abuse and presents a good discussion of the effects of beginning parenthood at different ages (adolescence, early twenties, and middle life) on the development of the family. The effects and treatment of sexual abuse are covered. The approach of the legal system in both the United States and Europe is explained.

O'Brien, Shirley. **Child Abuse: A Crying Shame.** Provo, UT: Brigham Young University Press, 1980. 198p.

Written for parents, educators, day-care workers, students, and friends of children everywhere, this book includes definitions, statistics, and information on types of abuse, abusers, legal protection, and prevention. Neglect is covered in some detail. The text of Public Law 93-247, the Child Abuse Prevention Act, is also included.

Office of Justice Assistance, Research, and Statistics. **How To Protect Children: Take a Bite Out of Crime.** Washington, DC: Government Printing Office, 1984.

This publication for young people has almost a cartoon appearance. It gives information on when to suspect that someone is planning to molest you and where to call for help. Attractive and easy to read.

U.S. Congress. House. **Children, Youth, and Families: A Year-End Report on the Activities of the Select Committee on Children, Youth, and Families.** Washington, DC: Government Printing Office, 1984.

The background of the child abuse problem is given through expert testimony, including reactions to proposed legislation. Costs, unemployment, and pregnancy of young adolescents are a few of the topics covered.

U.S. Congress. House Committee on Children, Youth, and Families. **Violence and Abuse in American Families. 98th Congress.** Washington, DC: Government Printing Office, 1984.

Prepared statements of expert witnesses and government officials concerned with the problem.

U.S. Congress. Senate Subcommittee on Juvenile Justice of the Committee on the Judiciary. **Relationship between Child Abuse, Juvenile Delinquency, and Adult Criminality. 98th Congress.** Washington, DC: Government Printing Office, 1983.

Expert witnesses and authorities are quoted from their testimony.

U.S. Department of Health and Human Services. **Adolescent Maltreatment: Issues and Program Models.** DHHS Publication No. (OHDS) 84-30339. Washington, DC: Government Printing Office, 1984.

This publication grew out of a cluster of projects funded by the National Center on Child Abuse and Neglect. It is divided into three sections: (1) issues in adolescent maltreatment, (2) service models, and (3) past, present, and future perspectives.

————. **Child Abuse and Neglect Litigation, A Manual of Judges.** Washington, DC: Government Printing Office, 1981.

This manual focuses on the practical aspects of a judge's work in abuse and neglect cases. The facts and family dynamics for each case are unique and the judge must rely upon a fundamental understanding of child abuse and neglect, as well as the appropriate responses of both treatment agencies and the judicial system. The management of the court cases is also included: legal rights of involved parents, privacy of records, representation of the child, collecting of evidence and information, coping with the media and hysteria, court-ordered home supervision, removal from home, and termination of parental rights.

————. **Child Abuse and Neglect Publications.** Washington, DC: Government Printing Office, 1986.

The books, pamphlets, and kits in this list were reviewed and cataloged by the National Advisory Board on Child Abuse and Neglect and are offered by the Board for use as professional and community resources. All articles were carefully screened.

————. **Child Sexual Abuse: Incest, Assault, and Sexual Exploitation.** Washington, DC: Government Printing Office, 1979.

Effects of sexual abuse on children and families are discussed, as well as intervention and the legal response to child sexual abuse. Procedures to prevent and treat sexual abuse are included, along with a bibliography and references.

————. **How To Plan and Carry Out a Successful Public Awareness Program on Child Abuse and Neglect.** Washington, DC: Government Printing Office, 1977.

The goals of the public relations campaign outlined in this book are (1) to increase knowledge about child abuse and neglect, and (2) to apply that knowledge to improve and expand prevention and treatment efforts. Practical suggestions for radio spots, television, newspapers, and direct mail are included.

————. **Selected Readings on Adolescent Maltreatment.** DHHS Publication No. (OHDS) 81-30301. Washington, DC: Government Printing Office, 1981.

The document contains 11 papers that discuss aspects of the maltreatment of adolescents, with particular emphasis on definition and incidence, models of adolescent development, and intervention techniques. The papers were selected to provide broad coverage of the issues.

————. **Working Together: A Plan To Enhance Coordination of Child Abuse and Neglect Activities.** Washington, DC: DHHS publication, 1980. 42p.

Recommendations include: (1) Develop community-based comprehensive plans for preventing child abuse and neglect. (2) Bring to the attention of federal, state, and local child abuse and neglect programs the needs of the abused and neglected child within the context of the family. (3) Stimulate activities to improve state and local child protective services. (4) Stimulate voluntary sector research, service delivery, and advocacy for the prevention and treatment of child abuse and neglect. (5) Improve communication and cooperation among federal agencies involved in child abuse and neglect activities. (6) Maintain the National Center on Child Abuse and Neglect leadership role as educator and technical assistance provider, both in coordinating child abuse and neglect activities at the federal level and in improving the capacity of public and private agencies to respond to the problem.

U.S. Department of Health, Education, and Welfare. **Resource Materials: A Curriculum on Child Abuse and Neglect.** Washington, DC: Government Printing Office, 1979.

Divided into two parts and eight units, this document covers topics such as child protective intervention, the role of the courts in child abuse and neglect, identifying the physicially abused child, and building skills in dealing with families.

Whitcomb, Debra, Elizabeth R. Shapiro, and Lindsey D. Stellwagen. **When the Victim is a Child: Issues for Judges and Prosecutors.** Washington, DC: National Institute of Justice, 1985.

An introduction to the problem of child victims is followed by a section on innovative practices, legal issues and practical concerns, and use of expert witnesses and victim advocates.

ARTICLES

Adams-Tucker, Christine. **"Defense Mechanisms Used by Sexually Abused Children,"** *Children Today* 14, no. 1 (January/February 1985): 8–12.

The author discusses in psychological terms some of the behaviors adopted by sexually abused children.

Beck, Melinda. **"An Epidemic of Child Abuse,"** *Newsweek* 104, no. 8 (20 August 1984): 44.

The author expresses concern for the escalation of reported child abuse incidents, with a focus on the alleged abuses at the McMartin Pre-School in Manhattan Beach, California.

Brenner, Avis. **"Wednesday's Child,"** *Psychology Today* 19, no. 5 (May 1985): 46–50.

Brenner defines neglect, speculates about its possible causes, and lists its symptoms, both physical and behavioral.

Finkelhor, David. **"How Widespread Is Child Sexual Abuse?"** *Children Today* 13, no. 4 (July/August 1984): 18–20.

Through surveys and extrapolation of data, estimates are made about the prevalance of sexual abuse. Limitations on data are examined.

Fontana, Vincent J. **"When Systems Fail: Protecting the Victim of Child Sexual Abuse,"** *Children Today* 13, no. 4 (July/August 1984): 14–18.

Using a broad definition of systems, the author surveys the medical, educational, and legal aspects in a community.

Hittleman, Margo. **"Sexual Abuse: Teaching about Touching,"** *School Library Journal* 31, no. 5 (January 1985): 34–35.

After giving background on different kinds of touching, the author suggests books that deal with sexual abuse and how young people can deal with it.

Leo, John. **"Some Day I'll Cry My Eyes Out,"** *Time* 123, no. 17 (23 April 1984): 72–73.

Reports on the alleged incidents of child molestation at the McMartin Pre-School in Manhattan Beach, California, and on related cases elsewhere.

VanMeter, Vandelia L. **"Family Violence and Child Abuse: A Bibliography of Audiovisual Materials,"** *The Book Report,* November/December 1986, 61–63.

Welsh, Ralph S. **"Spanking: A Grand Old American Tradition?"** *Children Today* 14, no. 1 (January/February 1985): 25–29.

Based on his research, the author discusses the definition of spanking, its frequency and long-term effects. He concludes spanking is a serious matter that leads to more violence in our society.

Zigler, Edward, and Nancy Rubin. **"Why Child Abuse Occurs,"** *Parents* 60, no. 11 (November 1985): 102–106, 215–218.

The authors explore the reasons for child abuse and conclude stress, isolation, and ignorance are major causes.

Nonprint Materials on Child Abuse

Barb: Breaking the Cycle of Child Abuse

Type:	16mm color film
Length:	28 min.
Cost:	Rental $50, purchase $395
Distributor:	Motorola Teleprograms
	4825 North Street
	Schiller Park, IL 60176
Date:	1978

This dramatization shows how anger and a poor self-image resulting from a neglected childhood can lead to violent behavior as a parent.

Battered Teens

Type:	16mm color film
Length:	11 min.
Cost:	Rental $40, purchase $250
Distributor:	Films Inc.
	5547 N. Ravenswood Avenue
	Chicago, IL 60640-1199
Date:	1981

A family attempts to break the chain of child abuse through self-help groups for the parents and the abused teenager.

Because They Love Me
Type: 16mm color film or video
Length: 31 min.
Cost: Purchase $495 (film), $370 (video)
Distributor: Coronet Films and Video
              108 Wilmot Road
              Deerfield, IL 60015-9990
Date: 1980

A dramatization of the effect of emotional abuse on two young girls.

The Best Kept Secret
Type: 16mm color film or video
Length: 15 min.
Cost: Rental $50, purchase $275 (film); purchase $250 (video)
Distributor: Motorola Teleprograms
              4825 North Street
              Schiller Park, IL 60176
Date: 1984

Produced by ABC for the "20/20" television program, this film examines the 1984 case in which seven teachers were accused of child molestation at a preschool. It also looks at the responsibilities of parents and the community for ensuring the safety of children. Journalistic assumptions of guilt and innocence are examined.

Better Safe Than Sorry
Type: 16mm color film
Length: 19 min.
Cost: Rental $40, purchase $395
Distributor: Vitascope Film Fair Communications
              10900 Ventura Boulevard
              Studio City, CA 91604
Date: 1985

The concept of individual responsibility for safety is highlighted through stories of teens in three situations: (1) a date rape, (2) incest with the father, and (3) a boy's near molestation by a coach. Rights of teens and ways to avoid such predicaments are discussed.

Breaking Silence
Type: 16mm color film or video
Length: 58 min.
Cost: Purchase $800 (film), $250 (video)

Distributor: Future Educational Films
1414 Walnut #4
Berkeley, CA 94709
Date: 1986

A compassionate look at child abuse through the eyes of molestation victims and one offender. Common threads run through the stories: guilt, learning to trust, and breaking the cycle of abuse.

Cheryl
Type: Video
Length: 15 min.
Cost: Purchase $350
Distributor: CBS Broadcast
51 W. 52nd Street
New York, NY 10019
Date: 1984

Originally a segment on the "60 Minutes" television program, this is the true story of a sexually abused child, whose father denies wrongdoing and whose mother is treated as a troublemaker when she tries to keep the child away from the father, whom she has divorced.

Child Abuse: Breaking the Cycle
Type: 3 filmstrips
Length: 39 min.
Cost: Purchase $129 (set of 3)
Distributor: Sunburst
39 Washington Avenue
Pleasantville, NY 10570
Date: 1982

Filmed at a Parents Anonymous meeting, Child Abuse: Breaking the Cycle discusses the causes of child abuse and ways to stop it.

Child Abuse: Cradle of Violence
Type: 16mm color film
Length: 22 min.
Cost: Rental $50 per week, purchase $375
Distributor: Motorola Teleprograms
4825 North Street
Schiller Park, IL 60176
Date: 1976

The film demonstrates parental frustrations leading to violence and stresses the importance of parenting courses and self-help groups in combatting these frustrations.

Child Abuse—Don't Hide the Hurt
Type: 16mm color film
Length: 12 min.
Cost: Rental $25
Distributor: AIMS Media
               6901 Woodley Avenue
               Van Nuys, CA 91406-4878
Date: 1978

A dramatization of a young boy victimized by his father, presenting the reality of child maltreatment to his classmates.

Child Abuse: The People Next Door
Type: 16mm color film
Length: 20 min.
Cost: Rental $36, purchase $360
Distributor: Barr Films
               P.O. Box 7878
               12801 Schabarum Avenue
               Irwindale, CA 91706-7878
Date: 1980

A woman abandoned by her husband and left alone with two small children begins to take out her frustrations on the children until she receives counseling.

Child Abuse and the Law
Type: 16mm color film or video
Length: 27 min.
Cost: Purchase $360 (film), $110 (video)
Distributor: Perennial Education, Inc.
               930 Pitner
               Evanston, IL 60202
Date: 1979

An attorney and a pediatrician instruct teachers on identifying and helping child abuse victims. Recommended for in-service programs.

Child Sexual Abuse: What Your Children Should Know
Type: 16mm color film or video
Length: 30 min. (separate programs for grades K–3 and 7–12)
Cost: Purchase $635 (film), $250 (video)
Distributor: Indiana University AudioVisual Center
               Bloomington, IN 47401
Date: 1984

The program for grades 7–12, through dramatization of threatening situations, offers topics for discussion ranging from a preoccupation with the opposite sex to acquaintance rape and incest.

Children in Peril
Type: 16mm color film
Length: 22 min.
Cost: Purchase $335
Distributor: Xerox Films, Inc.
                245 Long Hill Road
                Middletown, CT 06457
Date: 1972

Statistics are provided on the incidence of child abuse and neglect, and experts in the field discuss the causes, the psychology of abusive parents, and legal aspects.

Cum Laude, Cum Lonely
Type: 16mm color film
Length: 27 min.
Cost: Rental $35
Distributor: Media Guild
                11722 Sorrento Valley Road, Suite E
                San Diego, CA 92121
Date: 1976

A depiction of the emotional impact of parental uninterest on a young man.

Do I Have To Kill My Child?
Type: 16mm color film
Length: 52 min.
Cost: Rental $12.50, purchase $572
Distributor: Australian Information Service
                636 Fifth Avenue
                New York, NY 10020
Date: 1976

A young mother is unable to cope with daily stress, resulting in child abuse. Her pleas for help are ignored by her husband, doctor, mother, and neighbor.

Don't Give Up on Me
Type: 16mm color film
Length: 28 min.
Cost: Rental $50 per week, purchase $375

Distributor: Motorola Teleprograms
                  4825 North Street
                  Schiller Park, IL 60176
Date: 1975

The viewer is taken from the initial report of abuse through the court hearing and treatment for the family. Includes a manual that is helpful for discussion and follow-up. Available in a Spanish version.

Family Affair
Type: 16mm film or video
Length: 28 min.
Cost: Rental $75, purchase $450 (film); rental $75 (video)
Distributor: Visucom Productions, Inc.
                  1255 Veterans Boulevard
                  Redwood City, CA 94063
Date: 1981

Ed Asner narrates this award-winning film that shows the effect of spousal abuse on the children. The legal and victim advocate systems are explained.

Family Violence in America: The Conspiracy of Silence
Type: 16mm film or video
Length: 28 min.
Cost: Rental $50, purchase $425 (film); purchase $425 (video)
Distributor: FMS Productions
                  1777 N. Vine Street
                  Los Angeles, CA 90028
Date: 1982

An introduction to the problems of physical and verbal abuse affecting couples, both as marriage partners and as parents.

Fragile: Handle with Care
Type: 16mm color film
Length: 26 min.
Cost: $125/free on request
Distributor: Independent Order of Foresters
                  100 Border Avenue, Suite B
                  Solana Beach, CA 92075
Date: 1974

Three actual cases of child abuse are reenacted, beginning with the funeral of an abused child and the mother describing the incidents that led to the death.

The Hidden Crime

Type: Various video formats
Length: 16 min.
Cost: Purchase, no amount indicated
Distributor: Media Guild
               11722 Sorrento Valley Road, Suite E
               San Diego, CA 92121
Date: 1979

This factual program provides ample proof of the grim reality of incest in our society. The characters are not actors, but real people who discuss how it happened and what the effects were. Produced for CBS News series "Magazine." Support materials available.

Home Sweet Home

Type: 16mm color film
Length: 15 min.
Cost: Purchase $150
Distributor: National Instructional Television Center
               Box A, 1111 W. 17th Street
               Bloomington, IN 47401
Date: 1973

A comparison of two boys and their families designed to help students cope with feelings of mistreatment.

If It Happens to You

Type: 2 filmstrips with cassettes, teacher's guide
Length: 13 min.
Cost: Purchase $99
Distributor: Sunburst Communications
               36 Washington Avenue, Room CG
               Pleasantville, NY 10570
Date: 1985

A school counselor narrates a program showing children in various situations involving sexual abuse. Assertive responses are suggested.

Incest: The Broken Silence

Type: 3/4" video
Length: 30 min.
Cost: Purchase, no amount indicated
Distributor: KPBS
               15760 Ventura Boulevard, Suite 532
               Encino, CA 91436
Date: 1978

This documentary focuses on father-daughter incestuous relationships, showing through interviews the basic causes leading to incest, its effect on its victims, and possible solutions. Support materials available.

Incest: The Family Secret
Type:	Video
Length:	57 min.
Cost:	Rental $75, purchase $445
Distributor:	Filmmakers
	133 E. 58th Street
	New York, NY 10012
Date:	1979/1983

Exploring the causes and effects of incest, this Canadian documentary features honest discussion with victims and perpetrators.

Incest: The Victim Nobody Believes
Type:	3/4″ video
Length:	23 min.
Cost:	Rental or purchase, no amount indicated
Distributor:	MTI Teleprograms Inc.
	108 Wilmot Road
	Deerfield, IL 60015-9990
Date:	1978

This program helps make the public aware of the extent of this problem. Three young women openly discuss their experiences.

Interviewing the Abused Child
Type:	16mm color film
Length:	21 min.
Cost:	Rental $50, purchase $375
Distributor:	Motorola Teleprograms
	4825 North Street
	Schiller Park, IL 60176
Date:	1978

A doctor, a social worker, and a teacher conduct a total of five case interviews to demonstrate different techniques used by professionals in interviewing abused and neglected children.

It Shouldn't Hurt To Be a Kid
Type:	16mm color film or video
Length:	21 min.
Cost:	Rental $50, purchase $480 (film); purchase $360 (video)

Distributor: Aims Media
                 6901 Woodley Avenue
                 Van Nuys, CA 91406-4878
Date: 1985

This film is directed at Californians who work with youth and discusses their legal responsibilities. Useful to all persons in the helping professions.

Learning To Say No

Type: 2 filmstrips, 2 cassettes, 1 guide
Cost: Purchase $99 (complete package)
Distributor: Sunburst Communications
                 36 Washington Avenue, Room CG
                 Pleasantville, NY 10570
Date: 1984

Assertiveness training for intermediate and junior high school students.

Silent Neighbor

Type: 16mm color film
Length: 10 min.
Cost: Rental $15, purchase $150
Distributor: Film Comm
                 108 W. Grand Avenue
                 Chicago, IL 60610
Date: 1980

A capsule history of child abuse produced by the Association of Retarded Citizens. The film explains the responsibilities of neighbors and the community.

Socio-Drama

Type: 1/2" black and white video
Length: 20 min.
Cost: Free rental
Distributor: New Jersey Division of Youth and Family Services
                 1 S. Montgomery Street
                 Trenton, NJ 08652
Date: 1979

A high-school classroom skit examining the multi-problem aspects of child maltreatment while presenting the human side of the abusive parent.

The Summer We Moved to Elm Street

Type: 16mm color film
Length: 28 min.
Cost: Rental $20 per showing, purchase $405
Distributor: McGraw-Hill
                Education Resources
                P.O. Box 408
                Hight's Town, NJ 08520
Date: 1977

A 9-year-old girl's feelings are explored as she adjusts to a new neighborhood in the midst of problems caused by parental conflicts and a nonsupportive alcoholic father. Problems of a mobile society are presented.

Sweet Whispers, Brother Rush (2-part series)

Type: 2 filmstrips, 2 audiocassettes
Length: Part I: 20:57 min., Part II: 18:29 min.
Cost: Purchase $52 (complete package)
Distributor: McGraw-Hill
                Education Resources
                P.O. Box 408
                Hight's Town, NJ 08520
Date: 1983

Evocative drawings enhance Virginia Hamilton's narration of her Newbery Award Honor book. The brother and sister live by themselves, with the mother coming only occasionally between jobs.

Targets

Type: 16mm color film or video
Length: 19 min.
Cost: Rental $75, purchase $450 (film); purchase $350 (video)
Distributor: MTI Teleprograms
                108 Wilmot Road
                Deerfield, IL 60015-9990
Date: 1986

Explores personal violence, child molestation, peer pressure, and alcoholism.

Time for Caring: The School's Response to the Sexually Abused Child

Type: 16mm color film or video
Length: 28 min.
Cost: Rental $50, purchase $390 (film); purchase $390 (video)

Distributor: Lawren Productions
              12121 Pinewood Drive
              P.O. Box 666
              Mendocino, CA 95460
Date: 1979

Intended to help school personnel recognize the signs of sexual abuse and understand the school's responsibility in reporting the problem.

Twelve and a Half Cents

Type: 16mm color film or video
Length: 40 min.
Cost: Purchase $300 (film or video)
Distributor: Canadian Broadcasting Corp.
              1400 Dorchester Boulevard East
              Montreal, Quebec H2L 2M2
              Canada
Date: 1976

A dramatization of an abusive family situation that includes the contributing factors of marital strife and financial problems, abuse in the mother's background, inadequate follow-up by officials, and an eventual death.

Victims

Type: 16mm color film or video
Length: 24 min.
Cost: Rental $60, purchase $425 (film); rental $60, purchase $360 (video)
Distributor: Chuck Wintner
              22541-A Pacific Coast Highway, Suite 59
              Malibu, CA 90265
Date: 1981

Interviews with convicts, juvenile delinquents, and abusive parents clarify some of the causes of violent behavior. Recommended for parenting classes.

Violence in the Home: An American Tragedy

Type: Filmstrip with cassette
Length: 16 min.
Cost: Purchase $28 (complete package)
Distributor: Current Affairs Films
              P.O. Box 426
              Ridgefield, CT 06877
Date: 1977

This film gives information on the causes of child abuse and wife-beating in all social groups. Interviews disclose the feelings of both husband and wife.

Who Do You Tell?

Type:	16mm color film
Length:	11 min.
Cost:	Rental $25, purchase $195
Distributor:	Motorola Teleprograms
	4825 North Street
	Schiller Park, IL 60176
Date:	1977

An animated film encouraging children to talk about their problems.

Whose Child Is This?

Type:	16mm color film
Length:	28 min.
Cost:	Rental $40, purchase $400
Distributor:	Learning Corp.
	1350 Avenue of the Americas
	New York, NY 10102
Date:	1979

In this award-winning film, a teacher goes through the steps involved from first identifying Stephen as an abuse victim, through the legal steps used by the state of Kentucky to respond to child abuse.

Organizations Concerned with Child Abuse

The American Association for Protecting Children
9725 E. Hampden Avenue
Denver, CO 80231
(303) 695-0811
Executive Director: Ms. Patricia Schene

The American Humane Society was originally formed in 1877 to protect both children and animals. This division assists communities everywhere in developing new programs for protection of children or in improving programs already in existence. It emphasizes the political expression of citizens' views, researches child abuse, rates programs, and issues data on abused children.

Child Abuse Listening Mediation: CALM
P.O. Box 718
Santa Barbara, CA 93102
(805) 682-1366
Executive Director: Michael Long

A private, nonprofit organization, CALM has a hotline staffed chiefly by volunteer workers who are interested and dedicated people from throughout the community. The prime purpose is to quiet upset parents by listening sympathetically to them and helping them before harm is done. The caller is also provided with sources of professional help. CALM's volunteers are prepared to go into the homes in that area as listeners and "friendly neighbors."

PUBLICATION: *Calmword* newsletter (quarterly).

The Child Welfare League of America
440 First Street NW, #310
Washington, DC 20001
(202) 638-2952
Executive Director: David S. Liederman

An association of child welfare agencies in the United States and Canada, with main offices in Washington, D.C. Its basic aim is the constant improvement of welfare work being done for needy, abused, and neglected children. It works at setting high standards for welfare agencies to follow, consults with agencies, does research, and publishes a wide range of materials.

PUBLICATIONS: *Child Welfare* (bimonthly), *Children's Voice* (monthly), directory (annual), plus books, monographs, and newsletters.

National Committee for Prevention of Child Abuse
332 S. Michigan Avenue, Suite #950
Chicago, IL 60604
(312) 663-3520
Executive Director: Anne Harris Cohn

This group provides information for people who want to find solutions to child abuse, including sexual abuse. It stresses preventive efforts, gives referrals, and offers volunteer opportunities. Serves as a national advocate to prevent the neglect and physical, sexual, and emotional abuse of children.

PUBLICATIONS: Pamphlets and booklets.

National Exchange Club Foundation for the Prevention of Child Abuse (Child Welfare) (NECF)
3050 Central Avenue
Toledo, OH 43606
(419) 535-3232
Director of Foundation: George Mezinko

A project of the National Exchange Clubs, the foundation works through 37 centers throughout the United States to combat child abuse. The centers implement local programs that treat abusive parents. They also maintain a speakers' bureau and compile statistics.

PUBLICATIONS: Pamphlets and brochures.

Parents United International
P.O. Box 952
San Jose, CA 95108
(408) 280-5055
Executive Director: Dr. Henry Giarretto

Begun in Santa Clara County with social welfare workers, this organization has developed 160 chapters throughout the country, which are sponsored by an approved professional agency. There are three divisions within the organization: (1) Adults Molested as Children, (2) Daughters and Sons United, and (3) Parents United. Daughters and Sons United focuses on intrafamily relationships, especially incest, and works to alleviate the trauma experienced by the child. They also facilitate the abused child's awareness of his/her feelings. Parents United is a resource for sexual abuse victims, perpetrators, and families to call for referrals to local affiliates. They provide crisis and long-term support, encouraging self-help sessions in conjunction with other groups, such as Daughters and Sons United.

PUBLICATION: Newsletter (bimonthly).

Paul and Lisa
P.O. Box 348
Westbrook, CT 06498
(203) 399-5338
President: Frank N. Barnsba

This group serves as a national program for the prevention and rehabilitation of sexually abused children. The name came from the church that gave the seed money to start the program and from Lisa, a young girl who died after being sexually exploited. Paul and Lisa believes in educating the public, children, and professionals on the dangers of sexual abuse.

PUBLICATION: *Paul and Lisa Connection* (quarterly).

Victims Anonymous (Sexual Abuse)
9514-9 Reseda Boulevard, #607
Northridge, CA 91324
(818) 993-1139
Executive Director: Lori Brown

The goals of this organization are to dispell the myths and shame surrounding victims of sexual assault/abuse and families of victims. The group offers referrals and shelter to victims and their families and prepares child victims for court appearances. It also conducts seminars and workshops.

Hotlines and Resource Centers

Telephone numbers with an 800 prefix indicate there is no long-distance charge for the call.

CALM (805) 687-7912

Child Abuse Hotline—National (800) 422-4453

Parents Anonymous (800) 421-0353

Call your local police or sheriff's department if you have an emergency: 911 is the emergency number in most locations.

Index